C000070841

The Analyst and the Mystic

The *Analyst*

and the Mystic

PSYCHOANALYTIC REFLECTIONS ON RELIGION AND MYSTICISM

Sudhir Kakar

The University of Chicago Press

Sudhir Kakar is a distinguished psychoanalyst with a private practice in New Delhi. He is also a training analyst of the Indian Psychoanalytic Society and a visiting professor in the Department of Psychology and the Divinity School at the University of Chicago. His previous books include *The Inner World, Intimate Relations* and *Shamans, Mystics and Doctors.*

The University of Chicago Press, Chicago 60637
Penguin Books India (P) Ltd., New Delhi, India
© 1991 by The University of Chicago
All rights reserved. Published 1991
Printed in the United States of America
99 98 97 96 95 94 93 92 91 54321

Typeset by IPP Catalog Publications (P) Ltd., New Delhi, India

Library of Congress Cataloging-in-Publication Data
Kakar, Sudhir
     The analyst and the mystic: psychoanalytic reflections on
religion and mysticism / Sudhir Kakar.
        p.   cm.
     Presented as the 1990 Haskell lectures at the University of
Chicago Divinity School.
     Includes bibliographical references and index.
     ISBN 0–226–42283–6 (alk. paper)
     1. Psychoanalysis and religion.   2. Mysticism—Psychology.
     3. Mysticism—Hinduism.   4. Ramakrishna, 1836–1886—Psychology.
     5. Gurus—India—Psychology.   6. Psychotherapy—
     Religious aspects—Hindus.
     7. Psychology, Religious—India.   8. Freud, Sigmund, 1856–1939.
     I. Title.   II. Title: Haskell lectures.
     BF 175.5.R44K35   1991   90—29159
     291.4'22'019–dc20   CIP

♾ The paper used in this publication meets the minimum requirements of the American National Standard for information Sciences—Permanence of Paper for Printed Library Materials, ANSI Z39.48-1984.

For
Wendy Doniger
in friendship and admiration

Contents

Preface

Two years ago, I was invited by the Divinity School of the University of Chicago to deliver its Haskell Lectures in the area of comparative religion. I accepted this invitation with alacrity. It encouraged me to return to a field which I had reconnoitered in an earlier work on the healing function of religion and of such religious "functionaries" as shamans and mystics. After a decade-long intellectual exploration into the vagaries of sexual love, I welcomed the chance to once again engage with this other major area of human transcendence.

In retrospect, it seems inevitable that the focus of these lectures would be ecstatic mysticism, which signifies both a continuity with and departure from my preceding preoccupation with eroticism. Like the lover, the emotional mystic too strives for the transcendence of personal boundaries in an ineffable union with the other, though in case of the latter the other is spelled with a capital "O." The fervor of erotic passion, we know, only recognizes the spontaneity of religious passion as its equal and, in some cultures and at certain historical periods, even as its superior. I thus came to ecstatic, emotional mysticism with a curious sense of familiarity which I hoped would permit me access to its strangeness.

Mysticism for me is not something that lies outside the vast spaces of the human mind. Its insights, experiences, and yearnings are a heritage of our condition as human beings; they are a part of our humanity. Shorn of religious trappings, the mystical quest is not apart from the dailiness of life but pervades and informs life in its deepest layers.

I have approached the mystic as a psychoanalyst approaches a subject in the clinical encounter, with empathy, respect, and a sense of the complexity and wonder of human life. My intention has not been to pursue any reductionistic agenda, to "shrink" the mystic, but rather to expand our understanding of his mystery and, ultimately, of the working of our own selves. Of course, given the nature of my discipline, the understanding of mysticism and mystical experiences I aim for is necessarily in a psychological mode. The psychological understanding, I hope, complements other kinds of understanding; it does not replace them. A psychological appropriation of mysticism is certainly not the intention of these reflections. Yet, if my endeavor, like those of the analysts before me, brings the mystic down from the level of "divine" to that of human, I console myself with the thought that it may also help in raising the rest of us by making us more aware of our own sensuous and psychic potentials.

Traditionally, psychoanalysis has viewed art and science as valuable sublimatory creations. On the other hand, it has often seen in mysticism in particular and religion in general a regressive return to the protective beings (and being) of infancy and early childhood. Mysticism, I try to show in this book, is a radical enhancement of the capacity for creative experiencing, of the ability to experience "with all one's heart, all one's soul, and all one's might." It requires that the mystic undergo a creative immersion in the deepest layers of his or her psyche, with its potential risk of phases of chaos and lack of integration. The mystical regression is akin to that of the analysand, an absorbing and at times painful process at the service of psychic transformation. It differs from most analyses in that the regression is deeper. Where the mystical ability to experience profoundly is sought to be enhanced within a master-disciple relationship, as in most schools of Hinduism, Buddhism, and Sufism, the potential mystic may be better placed than the analysand to connect with—and perhaps correct—the depressive core at the base of human life which lies beyond language. Psychically, he or she is also more endangered. Mystical techniques in the master-disciple relationship, compared to those of psychoanalysis, are thus designed to foster radical regression, and the role of the master—*guru, pir, roshi*—is better understood by taking recourse to the concepts of the more "relational" analysts such as Donald Winnicott and Heinz Kohut, rather than by remaining within the paradigm of classical psychoanalytic theory with its motivational emphasis on drives and defenses.

The illustrative examples for my arguments are preeminently drawn from the Hindu religious tradition. Following a time-honored psychoanalytic usage where one strives for an in-depth understanding of a single case history in the hope that it may later prove to be representative for a host of other similar cases, I have tried to organize my observations and understanding of mysticism around the person of a single mystic, the nineteenth-century Hindu saint, Shri Ramakrishna.

I have sought to discuss in detail three interacting factors in his story—particular life historical experiences, the presence of a specific artistic or creative gift, and a facilitating cultural environment—which I believe may well go into the making of a mystic, at least of the ecstatic variety.

The first chapter of this book was also presented as an invited talk to the Canadian Psychoanalytic Association in Montreal. The comments of my Canadian colleagues were most helpful. I am especially thankful to the discussant of the paper, Dr. Eva Lester, for her helpful input which I have incorporated gratefully into the text.

1

Ramakrishna and the Mystical Experience

Of the many ways of inner transformation known to man, the mystical path is perhaps one of the most ancient, universal, and highly regarded, even when its practitioners have often lived in an uneasy truce, if not in frank antagonism, with the established religions of their societies.

The mystical path may be one but has many forks. Scholars of religion have distinguished them in various ways. Nathan Söderblom talks of "mysticism of the infinite," an elevation of awareness where the unifying experience with the suprahuman eliminates perception of the concrete and abstract elements from the sensate world. He contrasts this to "mysticism of personal life" where the experience is not rooted in ecstatic rapture, but in a meeting with God in the midst of life's problems and struggles, a meeting experienced at a deep level of faith within normal waking consciousness.[1] Martin Buber and John of the Cross would be two exemplars of Söderblom's mysticism of personal life. Of course, such distinctions are more sign posts rather than sharp dividers since shades of both "infinity" and "personality" will exist in every mystic.

Mysticism of the "infinite," my own focus of interest, has also been variously categorized—nature mysticism, theistic mysticism, and monistic or soul mysticism—although it is doubtful whether the categories are any different at the level of inner experience. Yet another distinction is the one made by William James between sporadic and cultivated mysticism, which corresponds to Arthur Deikman's separation between untrained-sensate and trained-sensate mystical experiences.[2] Ramakrishna was, of course, a "career" mystic, and though his initial forays into mysticism may have been sporadic and untrained, the latter half of his life was marked by regular and frequent mystical experiences of the cultivated, trained-sensate kind.

A mystical experience may be mild, such as a contact with a "sense of Beyond" among completely normal people, or it may be extreme with ecstasies and visions. We know from survey studies that more or less mild mystical experiences are widespread, even in countries without an active mystical tradition and where the intellectual climate is not particularly conducive to mystical thought. In the United States, for instance, 35 percent of the respondents in a large sample study by Andrew Greeley in 1975 reported having mystical experiences, a finding which has been since confirmed by other, comparable studies. It is significant that those who had such experiences were more educated than the national average and in "a state of psychological well-being" unmarked by any obvious neurotic difficulties.[3]

My focus here, though, is mysticism of the extreme variety and especially ecstatic mysticism. Most dramatically manifested in visions and trances, psychologically it is characterized by an expansion of the inner world, by a consciousness suffusing the whole of the body from inside. The expanding consciousness also fills the external world which appears to be pervaded by a oneness of existence.

The overwhelming feeling is of the object of consciousness, the world, having at last become transparent and more real than its conventional reality. All of this is accompanied by heightened intrapsychic and bodily sensations, culminating in a great feeling of pleasure which eliminates or absorbs all other experience.[4] Variously called cosmic consciousness, peak experience (Maslow), *mahabhava*, ecstatic mystical experience seems to differ from one where consciousness and its object, the world, become one and subject-object differentiations vanish. The *samadhi* of the Hindus, *satori* of Zen masters, and *fana* of the Sufis are some of the terms for this particular mystical experience. Again these distinctions are not either/or categories, the former often leading to the latter, as in the case of Ramakrishna, though not all mystics need to have spanned the whole gamut of mystical experience, each with its specific degree of ineffability and noesis—the conviction of knowing.

We must also remember that Ramakrishna was an heir to the Hindu mystical tradition which in spite of many similarities to the mysticism of other religious faiths, also has its own unique context. First, mysticism is the mainstream of Hindu religiosity, and thus Hindu mystics are generally without the restraints of their counterparts in monotheistic religious traditions such as Judaism, Islam, and to a lesser extent, Christianity, where mystical experiences and insights must generally be interpreted against a given dogmatic theology.[5] A Hindu mystic is thus normally quite uninhibited in expressing his views and does not have to be on his guard lest these views run counter to the officially interpreted orthodoxy. Second, God as conceived in the monotheistic religions does not have the same significance in two major schools of Hindu mysticism. Upanishadic mysticism, for instance, is a quest for spiritual illumination wherein a person's deepest essence is discovered to be identical with the common source of all other animate and inanimate beings. Yogic mysticism strives to realize the immortality of the human soul outside time, space, and matter. Through intensive introspection and practice of disciplines that lead to mastery of senses and mental processes, it seeks to realize the experience of one's "soul" as an unconditioned, eternal being, distinct from the "illusory" consciousness of the conditioned being. In both Upanishadic and Yogic mysticism there is no trace of love of or yearning for communion with God, which is considered the highest manifestation of the mystical mood in both Christian and Islamic traditions and without which no *unio mystica* is conceivable. In these two Hindu schools, mystical liberation is achieved entirely through the mystic's own efforts and without the intervention of divine grace. It is only in *bhakti* or devotional mysticism—Ramakrishna's preferred form—where love for the Deity creeps in, where the mystic's soul or "self" is finally united with God (or Goddess) in an ecstatic surrender, that Hindu mysticism exhibits a strong family resemblance to the mysticism of monotheistic faiths.

Let me state at the outset that given the theoretical uncertainties in contemporary psychoanalysis which threaten its basic paradigm, the earlier equation of the mystical state with a devalued, if not pathological, regression comparable to a psychotic episode is ripe for radical revision. Many analysts interested in the phenomenon would now agree that in spite of superficial resemblances, the mystical retreat is neither as complete nor as compelling and obligatory as psychotic regression. Moreover, in contrast to the psychotic, the mystic's ability to maintain affectionate ties remains unimpaired when it does not actually get enhanced. Given the analyst's commitment to Freud's dictum that the capacity "to love and work" is perhaps the best outer criterium for mental health, then the mystic's performance on both counts is impressive—that is, if one can succeed in emancipating one's self from a circumscription of the notions of love and work dictated by convention. In short, the full force of the current flowing through the psyche that leads to short circuit in the psychotic may, and indeed does, illuminate the mystic.

Some of the more recent work in psychoanalysis recognizes that mystical states lead to more rather than less integration of the person.[6] The mystic's insight into the workings of his or her self is more rather than less acute. Although consciousness during the mystical trance may be characterized by "de-differentiation" (to use Anton Ehrenzweig's concept)[7], that is, by the suspension of many kinds of boundaries and distinctions in both the inner and outer worlds, its final outcome is often an increase in the mystic's ability to make ever-finer perceptual differentiations. In other words, the point is not the chaotic nature of the mystical experience, if it is indeed chaotic, but the mystic's ability to create supreme *order* out of the apparent chaos. In fact, what I would like to do here is address the question Romain Rolland, in writing of Ramakrishna's initial trances, posed for "physicians both of the body and of the mind," namely, "There is no difficulty in proving the apparent destruction of his whole mental structure, and the disintegration of its elements. But how were they reassembled into a synthetic entity of the highest order?"[8] To put it differently, how does the mystic become master of his madness and of his reason alike whereas the schizophrenic remains their slave?

The timing of my attempt to formulate some kind of answers to these questions is not inopportune. Today, psychoanalysis is in a relatively better position of *adequatio* (adequateness) in relation to mystical phenomena as well as other states of altered consciousness, such as the possession trance. The *adequatio* principle, of course, states that the same phenomenon may hold entirely different sets of meaning for different observers.[9] To a dog, a book belongs to a class of objects which can be played with but not eaten. To the illiterate, it may be just a book, ink markings on paper he cannot decipher. To the average educated adult, the book is an impenetrable scientific tome. To the physicist, the volume is a brilliant treatise on relativity which makes him question some of the ways he looks at the universe. In each case the level of meaning is a function of the *adequatio* of the observer. As far as mysticism is concerned, psychoanalysts today are neither dogs nor even illiterates but are, perhaps, just moving beyond the stage of the average educated adult.

The increase in the level of analytical *adequatio* has not come about because of any analyst's personal experience of training in the mystical disciplines (as far as I know). In part, this higher *adequatio* is due to the increased availability of analytically relevant information which is no longer limited to the writings or biographical and autobiographical accounts of a few Western mystics such as Teresa of Avila and John of Cross. In the last fifteen years, we have had access to psychodynamically informed interviews with members of mystical cults who have traveled varied distances on the mystical path and have experienced various states of altered consciousness, including the ecstatic trance.[10] In addition, we have at least two detailed case histories of intensive psychoanalytic therapy with patients who had both mystical proclivities and trance experiences.[11]

More than the availability of additional information, the greater *adequatio* of psychoanalysis in relation to mysticism stems from the work of many writers—Erik Erikson, Donald Winnicott, Wilfred Bion, and Jacques Lacan come immediately to my mind—who, in spite of their very different theoretical concerns, pursued a common antireductionistic agenda. The cumulative effect of their writings has been to allow the adoption of what Winnicott, in talking of transitional phenomena, called "a particular quality in attitude," with which I believe mystical states should also be observed. In other words, my own enhanced feeling of *adequatio* reflects the presence of an unstated project in contemporary psychoanalysis in which the copresence of different orders of experience is tolerated and no attempts are undertaken to explain one in terms of the other without reciprocity. As we shall see later, in their separate efforts to develop a phenomenology of creative experiencing, Winnicott, Lacan, and Bion are directly relevant for a reevaluation and reinterpretation of mystical phenomena.[12] Of the three, whereas Winnicott was more the poet, Lacan and Bion, in their explicit concern with questions of ultimate reality, its evolution and reflection in psychic life, may fairly be described as the mystics of psychoanalysis. (As someone who spent his childhood in India, it is quite appropriate that Bion is radically sincere in his approach to "O," his symbol for ultimate reality, whereas Lacan, I like to think, as befitting a Frenchman talking of the Real, is more an ironic mystic.)

The psychoanalytic understanding of any phenomenon begins with the narrative, with the echoes and reverberations of individual history. The individual I have selected for my own explorations is the nineteenth-century Bengali mystic Sri Ramakrishna. Together with Ramana Maharishi, Ramakrishna is widely regarded as the preeminent figure of Hindu mysticism of the last three hundred years, whatever preeminence may mean in the mystical context. He is a particularly apt choice for a psychoanalytic study of ecstatic mysticism since Freud's observations on the mystical experience, on what he called the "oceanic feeling," an omnibus label for all forms of extreme mystical experience, were indirectly occasioned by Ramakrishna's ecstasies.

It was the biography of Ramakrishna which Romain Rolland was working on at the time when he wrote to Freud in 1927, saying that though he found Freud's analysis of religion (in *The Future of a*

Illusion) juste, he would ideally have liked Freud to "make an analysis of spontaneous religious feelings, or more exactly, religious sensations which are entirely different from religion proper and much more enduring."[13] Rolland went to call this sensation oceanic, without perceptible limits, and mentioned two Indians who had such feelings and "who have manifested a genius for thought and action powerfully regenerative for their country and for the world.[14] Rolland added that he himself had all his life found the oceanic feeling to be a source of vital revival. Freud's response to Rolland, his analysis of the "oceanic feeling," was then spelled out in *Civilization and its Discontents.* It is highly probable that the term "oceanic feeling" itself is taken from Ramakrishna's imagery to describe the ineffable. For instance, one of Ramakrishna's oft-repeated metaphors is of the salt doll which went to measure the depth of the ocean: "As it entered the ocean it melted. Then who is there to come back and say how deep is the ocean?"[15]

Of course, ocean as a symbol for boundless oneness and unity in which multiplicities dissolve and opposites fuse not only goes back to the Upanishads in the Hindu tradition, but is one of the preferred metaphors of devotional mystics for the melting of ego boundaries in the Buddhist, Christian and Muslim traditions as well.[16] Christian mystics, for instance, have been greatly fond of the metaphor. "I live in the ocean of God as a fish in the sea."

Freud's response to Ramakrishna, as generally to "Mother India," was of unease. Although of some professional interest, Ramakrishna's florid ecstasies were as distant, if not distasteful, to his sensibility as the jumbled vision of flesh, the labyrinth flux of the animal, human, and divine in Indian art. In his acknowledgement of Rolland's book about Ramakrishna, Freud writes, "I shall now try with your guidance to penetrate into the Indian jungle from which until now an uncertain blending of Hellenic love of proportion, Jewish sobriety, and Philistine timidity have kept me away. I really ought to have tackled it earlier, for the plants of this soil shouldn't be alien to me; I have dug to certain depths for their roots. But it isn't easy to pass beyond the limits of one's nature."[17]

We are, of course, fortunate that the last four years of Ramakrishna's life, from 1882 to 1886, were recorded with minute fidelity by a disciple, Mahendranath Gupta, or M. as he called himself with modest self-effacement.[18] In the cases of most mystics throughout history, we have either had to rely on doctrinal writing that is formal and impersonal, or on autobiographical accounts from which intimate detail, considered trifling from transcendental heights, has been excised. M., on the other hand, with the obsessive fidelity of a Bengali Boswell, has left an enormously detailed chronicle of the daily life and conversations of Ramakrishna—his uninhibited breaking out in song and dance, his frequent and repeated ecstasies, his metaphysical discourses full of wisdom and penetrating insight, his parables, jokes, views, anxieties, and pleasures, the times he slept and ate and what he ate—which is rare in hagiographical literature. Let me then begin with the outer scaffolding of the story, a brief narration of events of Ramakrishna's early life. And though we can never know what *really* happened in his or anyone else's infancy and childhood, the former forever beyond the reach of memory, I have no hesitation in extending a qualified belief to Ramakrishna's own version of his life story. Yet, of course, it is not solely his version. As a reteller of his tale, I cannot help but also bring to bear a psychoanalytic sensibility in the choice of events I emphasize and others that I must have underplayed. The biographies by his direct disciples, on the other hand, are shaped by the traditional Hindu religious idiom, while the narration by Romain Rolland is molded by his more universalistic, spiritual concerns, in the sense of what Aldous Huxley called the "perennial philosophy."

Ramakrishna was born in 1836 in a Brahmin family in the village of Kamarpukur in Bengal. The parents were pious and very poor, but what I find exceptional about them in the context of nineteenth-century village India is their ages at the time of Ramakrishna's birth. At a time when the average longevity was less than thirty years, maternal death during childbirth fairly common, and the sexually reproductive years of the woman over by her early thirties, Ramakrishna's father was sixty-one and his mother forty-five years old when he was born. In the family there was a brother thirty-one years older, a sister twenty-seven years older, and another brother eleven years older. Yet another sister was born when Gadhadhar, that was his given name, was four years old.

Ramakrishna later remembered his mother Chandra as a simple soul without a trace of worldliness who could not even count money. She said whatever came to her mind, without obfuscation or concealment, and people even called her a "simpleton." Devoted to her youngest son, the fruit of old loins, she was nevertheless, as elderly parents often tend to be, inordinately anxious about any harm befalling him when he was not within her ken. A curious and lively child, intent on exploring the world, Ramakrishna did not exactly help in allaying his mother's anxieties. She sought to master these by daily prayers to the family deity wherein she besought the continued welfare of her little boy.

Perhaps Ramakrishna's later anxiousness whenever he was physically incapacitated, his almost hypochondriacal concerns at such times, can be directly traced to the elderly mother's anxieties about her youngest son.

The incident given as an example of the boy's willfulness, which sometimes ignored the conventional rules of conduct, concerns his hiding behind a tree and peeping out at women while they washed clothes and bathed at the village tank. One of the women complained to Chandra who then admonished the boy that all women were the same as his mother. Shaming them was shaming her, insulting their honor was insulting hers. We are told that the mortified boy never again repeated his behavior. To us post-Freudians, the incident embodies a child's natural sexual curiosity which the mother dampens by associating it with incestuous anxiety. Interestingly, in later life, Ramakrishna would use a mythological version of this personal experience, wherein the incestuous urgings and fears are much more explicit, to explain a part of his attitude toward women. One day, during his childhood, the god Ganesha saw a cat which, as some boys are apt to do, he proceeded to torture in various ways till the cat finally made its escape. When Ganesha came back home he saw to his surprise the bruises and marks of torture on his mother's, the goddess Parvati's body. The mother revealed to her son that all living beings in female form were part of her and whatever he did to any female he did unto his mother. On reaching marriageable age, Ganesha, lest he marry his mother, decided to remain a celibate forever. "My attitude to women is the same," was Ramakrishna's final comment.[19]

Khudiram, Ramakrishna's father, was a gentle man who is reported to have never scolded his son. He took a quiet pride in the boy's evident intelligence and phenomenal memory, which were further displayed to advantage when he started attending the village school at the age of five. However, though good at school (but bad at arithmetic), what the boy most enjoyed was painting pictures and spending time with the village potters learning how to make clay images of gods and goddesses. The artistic streak in Ramakrishna was strongly developed, and it seems appropriate that his first ecstasy was evoked by the welling up of aesthetic emotion; an episode of "nature" mysticism, it was the consequence of an aesthetically transcendent feeling: "I was following a narrow path between the rice fields. I raised my eyes to the sky as I munched my rice. I saw a great black cloud spreading rapidly until it covered the heavens. Suddenly at the edge of the cloud a flight of snow white cranes passed over my head. The contrast was so beautiful that my spirit wandered far away. I lost consciousness and fell to the ground. The puffed rice was scattered. Somebody picked me up and carried me home in his arms. An access of joy and emotion overcame me. . . . This was the first time that I was seized with ecstasy." [20]

Ramakrishna's father, who had been ill for awhile, died when the boy was around eight years of age. The effect of the father's death was to make Ramakrishna withdrawn and fond of solitude. His attendance at school became fitful. He drew closer to his mother and spent much time in helping her with her household duties and her daily prayers to the gods. He became very fond of listening to discourses on spiritual matters and spent hours at a pilgrimage house where wandering ascetics found a bed for a night or two before they resumed their wanderings. The latter activity alarmed his mother who feared that her son might decide to leave home and embrace the renunciant's life.

There were other fainting spells, as on the way to the temple of a goddess or when acting the part of Shiva in a play he lost all external consciousness. He later attributed these states to spiritual stirrings although his family suspected a physical malady and refrained from forcing him to go to school which by now he quite disliked.

The gradually deteriorating condition of the family after Khudiram's death worsened with the marriage of Ramakrishna's second brother. With the advent of the new daughter-in-law, quarrels and bickerings in the household increased markedly, a situation which the family's worsening economic circumstances, driving it to the edge of subsistence, did not help improve. The daily clamor and strife, I imagine, perhaps added its own impetus in pushing the sensitive and artistic boy more and more away from the distasteful discord of everyday reality and toward transcendental, spiritual matters and religious life. The latter too coursed through the village, as it does to great extent even today in rural India, in a powerful stream. There were the many rituals in which everyday life was embedded, frequent recitals from the Puranas, and the religious plays and festivals in which Ramakrishna participated by singing and dancing with fervid abandon. And, above all, there were the sudden inward, abstracted states, brought on at the oddest of times by outer stimuli such as listening to a song in praise of a god or to snatches of devotional music.

The young daughter-in-law died in childbirth when Ramakrishna was thirteen years old, and the burden of running the household once again fell on the aging shoulders of Ramakrishna's mother. To help alleviate the poverty, his eldest brother left for Calcutta to run a small Sanskrit school. His position as the head of the family now devolved on Ramakrishna's second brother who was temperamentally disinclined to take over responsibilities for his siblings and was in any case much too busy scrounging around for work.

Thus at the beginning of adolescence, Ramakrishna was left to his own devices, without the paternal guiding voice of his father or eldest brother. School became even more occasional. When he was not an enthusiastic participant in the village's religious life, he was at home with his mother, helping her with household tasks and sharing with her the rhythm of her woman's days. The village women who dropped in on his mother for a visit during the day seem to have adopted him as one of their own. They would ask him to sing—he had a very sweet singing voice—or to tell stories from the Puranas, of which he had an enormous stock. He performed scenes from popular plays for their amusement, playing all the parts himself. He listened to their secrets and woes and would attempt to lift the spirits of a dejected woman by acting out a rustic farce.

He loved putting on women's clothes and ornaments. Dressed thus, with a pitcher under his arm to fetch water from the tank like other village women, he would pass in front of the men and felt proud that no one suspected he was not a woman. Once, disguised as a poor weaver girl, he spent a whole evening in the closely guarded women's quarters of the village shopkeeper's house taking part in their conversation, without being discovered. In his mature years, talking to his disciples, there was a certain wry pride with which he related, and occasionally enacted to their surprised delight, incidents from his youth which showed his ability to mimic women's gestures and movements to perfection.

A fantasy from this period has Ramakrishna imagining that were he to be born again he would become a beautiful child widow with long black hair who would not know anyone else except Lord Krishna as a husband. The girl widow would live in a hut with an elderly woman as a guardian, a spinning wheel, and a cow which she would milk herself. During the day, after finishing household work, she would spin yarn, sing songs about Krishna, and after dusk ardently weep for the god, longing to feed him sweets made from the cow's milk. Krishna would come in secret, be fed by her and go away, his daily visits taking place without the knowledge of others.[21]

In the meantime, Ramakrishna's eldest brother Ramkumar was doing well in Calcutta, running his small school and performing religious services for some rich families. He called the seventeen-year-old Ramakrishna over to the city to assist him in his priestly duties.

Soon after, a new opportunity opened up when a rich woman built and consecrated a temple to the goddess Kali outside Calcutta and employed Ramkumar as its full-time priest. Ramkumar, who had been ailing for some time, found the task arduous and handed over his duties to Ramakrishna, the younger brother. He died a year later.

Ramkumar's death was to have a profound effect on Ramakrishna. Thirty-one years older, he had looked after Ramakrishna like a father after Khudiram's death. "Who can say," Ramakrishna's disciple-biographer asks, "how far his brother's death contributed to the kindling up of the fire of renunciation in the Master's pure mind, by producing in him a firm conviction about the transitoriness of the world?[22] In any case his behavior changed markedly as he became more and more engrossed in the worship of the Mother Goddess. As her priest he had to wake her up early in the morning, bathe and dress her, make garlands of flowers for her adornment. At nine he had to perform her worship, offer her food, and escort her to her silver bed at noon where she rested for the afternoon. Then came the evening worship. For Ramakrishna, these were no longer duties but heartfelt services. He became so absorbed in each one of them that he had to be reminded when it was time to go on to the next ritual.

After the closing of temple at midday and midnight, Ramakrishna shunned all company and disconsolately roamed around in the jungle at the edge of which the temple was located. All he yearned for with all his soul, he was to later tell us, was a vision, the personal *darshan* of the Mother. The spiritual thirst, the clinician would observe, was embedded in all the signs of a full-fledged depression. There was a great restlessness of the body, sleepless nights, loss of appetite in which eating was reduced to the bare minimum, eyes that filled up often and suddenly with tears. The nephew who looked after him became alarmed for his sanity when at night he saw Ramakrishna sitting under a tree naked, having flung off his clothes and even the sacred thread of a Brahmin, or, when he saw him put the leavings from leaf plates from which beggars had eaten to his mouth and to his head.

But now, as we come to a culmination of his "dark night of the soul," we need Ramakrishna's own words. "There was then an intolerable anguish in my heart because I could not have Her vision. Just as a man wrings a towel forcibly to squeeze out all the water from it, I felt as if somebody caught hold of my heart and mind and was wringing them likewise. Greatly afflicted by the thought that I might not have Mother's vision, I was in great agony. I thought that there was no use in living such a life. My eyes suddenly fell upon the sword that was in the Mother's temple. I made up my mind to put an end to my life with it that very moment. Like one mad, I ran and caught hold of it, when suddenly I had the wonderful vision of the Mother, and fell down unconscious. I did not know what happened then in the external world—how that day and the next slipped away. But in my heart of hearts, there was flowing a current of intense bliss, never experienced before. . . . It was as if the houses, doors, temples, and all other things vanished altogether; as if there was nothing anywhere! And what I saw was a boundless infinite conscious sea of light! However far and in whatever direction I looked, I found a continuous succession of effulgent waves coming forward, raging and storming from all sides with great speed. Very soon they fell on me and made me sink to the abysmal depths of infinity." [23]

Those familiar with mystical literature will recognize many elements in Ramakrishna's vision which are known to us from similar descriptions from all over the world, especially the feeling of being flooded by light. In the still controversial studies of near-death experiences, "seeing the light" and "entering the light" are said to be the deepest and most positive parts of that particular experience. The incident has not only universal but also cultural aspects. It is a very Hindu story of a man forcing the Goddess to appear by threatening to decapitate himself. This is an old theme, found both in religious and secular literature, for instance in the well-known story which has been so brilliantly retold for Western readers by Thomas Mann in his *The Transposed Heads*.

Unlike similar accounts of the first vision in the lives of most mystics, this particular vision, to which we will come back later and to which all his boyhood experiences seem like forerunners, was not sufficient to take him out of the "valley of the shadow of death." Its aftertaste but whetted an appetite for repeated blissful salvings. Even for the pious visitors to the temple, accustomed to a wide range in manifestation of religious fervor, Ramakrishna's behavior appeared bizarre. He would decorate his own person with the flowers and sandalwood paste brought for the worship of the goddess. He would feel the statue of the goddess breathing, try to feed her stony mouth, and carry on playful conversations as to who, the goddess or her priest, should eat first. Any diminution in the sense of her presence made him throw himself and roll violently on the ground, filling the temple with loud wailings at her absence. At such times his breath would almost stop, and he appeared to struggle for his very life. When he again received a vision of the goddess, he would beam with joy and become a different person altogether. The consensus of his employers and others was that he had become insane. Romain Rolland calls this a necessary period of hallucination, and even Ramakrishna referred to it as a passing phase of *unmada* (insanity), leaving it unambiguous— something he was not wont to do in respect of the visions in his later life—that the "madness" was less divine intoxication than human disintegration, however necessary it may have been as a prelude to the former. Later in life, he would wonder at some of his behavior during this phase—worshipping his own phallus as that of Shiva, being seized by ecstatic visions while he defecated, and so on.

The prescribed medical treatment for "insanity" did not have the desired effect. Finally, he was taken to his village home where his worried mother had him ministered to by both an exorcist and an Ayurvedic doctor. Slowly, he regained his normal state of health. To safeguard the apparent gains the family arranged his marriage, a step, which I know from professional experience, is even today considered as the best antidote to threatened or actual psychic breakdown. Of course, as far as Ramakrishna was concerned, there was never any question of the marriage being consummated. From the very beginning, in relation to his girl bride, he saw himself either as a woman or, in his ecstatic state, as a child. In the former case, the husband and wife were both girlfriends (*sakhis*) of the Mother Goddess while, in the latter, the wife was envisioned as the Goddess herself.

At the age of twenty-four, Ramakrishna, now accompanied by his wife, returned to Calcutta to resume his priestly duties at the Kali temple. There was a relapse in his condition, though in an attenuated form. Whereas his initial visions had been untutored and spontaneous, initiated by the passionate intensity of his longing for *darshan* of the Goddess, during the next eight years he systematically followed the prescribed practices laid down by the different schools of Hindu mysticism. The disciplines were undertaken under the guidance of different gurus who were amazed at his natural facility and speed in reaching the goal of *samadhi*, a capability they themselves had acquired only after decades of strenuous effort.

First, there were the esoteric meditations of Tantra, fierce and fearful, under the tutelage of a female guru, Brahmani Bhairavi. This was followed by the nondualistic way of Vedanta, of concentration and contemplation techniques which seek to discriminate the Real from the Non-Real, a discipline without the need for any divinity or belief in God, till in the attainment of the *samadhi* all distinctions between I and the Other vanish. Then there were the various ways of Vaishnava mysticism, full of love and devotion for Rama or Krishna, the incarnations of Vishnu, and of Shakta mysticism where the supreme deity is Shakti, the primordial energy and the great Mother Goddess. All of these, the Vaishnava and Shakta ways, are essentially affective, and to which he felt personally most attuned. Whatever the discipline, his mystical genius was soon recognized by laymen and experts alike. Disciples gathered. Pandits—the theologically learned—came to visit and to partake of his clear insight into the whole gamut of Hindu metaphysics, a product of lived experience rather than scriptural proficiency; in any conventional sense, he was more or less illiterate. Ramakrishna would convey this experience simply yet strikingly through devotional songs, Puranic myths, analogies, metaphors, and parables fashioned out of the concrete details of the daily life of his listeners. Most of all, they were attracted by his riveting presence, even when he absented himself in ecstatic trances many times a day, with a few lasting for several days.

The *samadhis* did not now come unbidden but when his constantly receptive state crossed a certain threshold either in song or abandoned dance, in contemplation of a natural phenomena or absorption in the image of a divinity. He had become both a great teacher and a great mystic without losing his childlike innocence and spontaneity, which extended well into his final days. At the end of his life, dying of throat cancer, his disciples pleaded with him to ask the Mother Goddess for an easing of his disease so that he could eat some solid food rather than continue to subsist on a little barley water which had been his only nourishment for six months. Ramakrishna reluctantly agreed. On the disciples' inquiry as to the fate of their request, Ramakrishna answered: "I said to the Mother, 'I cannot eat anything on account of this (showing the sore in his throat). Please do something that I can eat a little.' But the Mother said, 'Why? You are eating through all these mouths (showing all of you).' I could speak no more for shame." [24]

In my attempt to understand the meaning of Ramakrishna's inner states, let me begin with Ramakrishna's own version of his experience. Anthropologically speaking, I shall start with the "native's point of view" on the phenomenology of mystical states.

Although Ramakrishna had successfully practiced the "higher" Vedantic disciplines of monotheistic, soul-mysticism his own personal preference was for devotional, theistic mysticism of the Vaishnava and Shakta varieties. Ultimately, of course, both roads lead to the same destination. The impersonal soul of the Vedantic seer and the God or Mother Goddess—the primordial energy—of the devotee are identical, like fire and its power to burn. At first one may take the *neti, neti* (not this, not this) road of discrimination in which only Brahman is real and all else is unreal. Afterwards, the same person finds that everything in the universe, animate and inanimate, is God himself—he is both the reality and the illusion of the Maya. The negation is followed by an affirmation.

Ramakrishna felt that the classical disciplines of Yoga were very difficult to follow for most human beings since the identification of the self with the body, which these disciplines seek to undo, was too deeply embedded for any easy sundering. For those who could not get rid of the feeling of "I," it was easier to travel on the devotional path where one could instead cherish the idea that "I am God's servant" (or child, or friend, or mother, or lover, as the case may be). He illustrated this point through the example of the monkey god Hanuman, symbol of *dasa* (servant) devotionalism, who when asked by Rama, by God, how he looked at Him replied, "O Rama, as long as I have the feeling of "I," I see that you are the whole and I am a part; you are the Master and I am your servant. But when, O Rama, I have the knowledge of truth, then I realize that You are I and I am You." [25]

Even the passions—lust, anger, greed, inordinate attachment, pride, egoism—which have been traditionally held as obstacles to spiritual progress, do not need to be vanquished in devotional mysticism. The *vairagya*, the renunciation or rather the depassioning, can take place equally well by changing the object of these passions, directing them toward God rather than the objects of the world. "Lust for intercourse with the soul. Feel angry with those who stand in your way toward God. Be greedy to get Him. If there is attachment, then to Him; like *my* Rama, *my* Krishna. If you want to be proud, then be like Vibhishana [Ravana's brother in the epic of Ramayana] who says, "I have bowed before Rama and shall not bow to anyone else in the world." [26] Devotional mysticism does not demand an elimination of a sense of individual identity, of I-ness, which can instead be used to progress along the spiritual path. Thus in *vatsalya* devotionalism, the attitude of a mother toward God, Ramakrishna gives the example of Krishna's mother as the ideal to be emulated. "Yashoda used to think, 'Who will look after Gopala (Krishna's name as child) if *I* do not? He will fall ill if *I* do not look after him.' She did not know Krishna as God. Uddhava said to Yashoda, 'Mother, your Krishna is God Himself. He is the Lord of the Universe and not a common human being.' Yashoda replied, 'O who is talking about your Lord of the Universe? I am asking how *my* Gopala is. Not the Lord of the Universe, *my* Gopala.'" [27]

Ramakrishna's preferred mystical style did not need ascetic practices, yogic exercises, or a succession of ever more difficult meditations. What it required of the aspirant was, first, a recovery of a childlike innocence and freshness of vision, a renunciation of most adult categories. "To my Mother I prayed only for pure devotion. I said 'Mother, here is your virtue, here is your vice. Take them both and grant me only pure devotion for you. Here is your knowledge and here is your ignorance. Take them both and grant me only pure love for you. Here is your purity and here is your impurity. Take them both Mother and grant me only pure devotion for you. Here is your *dharma* (virtue) and here is your *adharma*. Take them both, Mother, and grant me only pure devotion for you.'" [28] And at another place, "Who can ever know God? I don't even try. I only call on him as Mother. . . . My nature is that of a kitten. It only cries 'Mew, mew.' The rest it leaves to the mother."

Being like a child in relation to the Divinity does not mean being fearful, submissive, or meek, but of existing in the bright-eyed confidence of continued parental presence and *demanding* its restoration when it is felt to be lacking or insufficient. "He is our Creator. What is there to be wondered if He is kind to us? Parents bring up their children. Do you call that an act of kindness? They must act that way. Therefore we should force our demands on God. He is our Father and Mother, isn't He? [29] Being a child, then, meant the joy of total trust, of being in the hands of infinitely powerful and infinitely beneficient forces. The power of this total trust is tremendous; its contribution to reaching the mystical goal vital. One of Ramakrishna's illustrative stories went that Rama who was God Himself had to build a bridge to cross the sea to Lanka. But the devotee Hanuman, trusting only in Rama's name, cleared the sea in one jump and reached the other side. He had no need of a bridge.

But perhaps the most important requirement of devotional mysticism, in all its varieties, was the intensity of the aspirant's yearning to be with God, whether in the dyad of mother-child, or as friend or as servant, or as lover. The longing had to be so intense that it completely took over body and mind, eliminating any need for performing devotions, prayers, or rituals. Ramakrishna illustrated this, his own yearning, through the parable of a guru who took his disciple to a pond to show him the kind of longing that would enable him to have a vision *(darshan)* of God. On coming to the pond, the guru pushed the disciple's head underwater and held it there. After a few seconds he released the disciple and asked, "How do you feel?" The disciple answered, "Oh, I felt as if I was dying! I was longing for a breath of air!" "That's exactly it," said the guru.[30] Like other kinds of mysticism, affective mysticism too has its developmental stages. Devotion *(bhakti)* matures into *(bhava)*, followed by *mahabhava, prema*, and then attainment of God in the *unio mystica*. Since the distinctions between *bhava, mahabhava* and *prema* seem to me to lie in their degrees of intensity rather than in any fundamental qualitative difference, let me try to understand the nature of only one of the three states, *bhava*, a term which Ramakrishna uses constantly to describe states of consciousness which preceded his visions and ecstatic trances.

Literally translated as "feeling," "mood," *bhava* in Vaishnava mystical thought means a state of mind (and body) pervaded with a particular emotion. Basing his illustrations of Hindu ideals, Ramakrishna lists the *bhavas* in relation to God as *shanta*, the serenity of a wife's devotion to her husband, *dasya*, the devoted submissiveness of the servant, *sakhya*, the emotion of friendship, *vatsalya*, the feeling of mother towards the child, and *madhurya*, the romantic and passionate feelings of a woman toward her lover. Ramakrishna felt that the last, symbolized in Radha's attitude toward Krishna, included all the other *bhavas*. Indeed, the discourse of passionate love is conducted in many *bhavas*. At times idealizing the lover makes "me" experience the loved one as an infinitely superior being whom I need outside myself as a *telos* to which or whom "I" can surrender and obey in *dasya*. At other times, there is the contented oneness of *vatsalya* as the lover becomes as a babe on the breast, not in quiescence, a complacence of the heart, but in voluptuous absorption and repose. At yet other times, there is the serene tranquility of *shanta*, the peace of the spouses in an ineffable intimacy, a state which the eighth-century Sanskrit poet Bhavabhuti lets Rama, with Sita asleep across his arm, describe as "this state where there is no twoness in response of joy or sorrow/where the heart finds rest; where feeling does not dry with age/where concealments fall away in time and essential love is ripened."[31] Besides the compulsions of possessive desire, all these *bhavas* too are at the core of man's erotic being.

Vaishnava mysticism, being a mysticism of love, does not consider awe as a legitimate *bhava* in relation to the Divine. Thus there are no feelings of reverence, of the uncanny, or of mystery. Nor are there the degrees of fear associated with awe where, in extremity, terror and dread can reign. Awe is perhaps the central *bhava* of what Erich Fromm called authoritarian religion. Vaishnava devotionalism, on the other hand, would consider awe as an obstacle in the mystical endeavor. It distances and separates rather than binds and joins.

I am aware that Ramakrishna's immersion in the various *bhavas* at different times in which he even adopted their outward manifestations can make him appear an outrageous figure to unsympathetic and prosaic observers. Practicing the *madhurya bhava* of Radha towards Krishna, he dressed, behaved, and lived as a girl for six months. At another time, going through the *dasya bhava* of Hanuman, he attached an artificial tail to his posterior in an effort to resemble the monkey god. When living in the motherly *bhava* of Yashoda toward Krishna, he had one disciple, who felt like a child toward him, lean against his lap as if suckling at his breast while the mystic talked or listened to the concerns of his other disciples.

I have mentioned *mahabhava* and *prema* as the higher, more intense states of *bhava* which most aspirants never manage to reach. *Mahabhava* shakes the body and mind to its very foundations, and Ramakrishna compared it to a huge elephant entering a small hut. *Prema*, on the other hand, which makes visions of the Divine possible, was in his analogy a rope by which one tethered God. Whenever one wanted a *darshan*, one had merely to pull the rope, and He appeared.

Psychologically speaking, I would tend to see *bhavas* as more than psychic looseners that jar the soul out of the narcissistic sheath of normal, everyday, self-limiting routine. They are experiences of extreme emotional states which have a quality of irradiation wherein time and space tend to disappear. We know of these feeling states from our experience of passionate love where, at its height, the loved one's beauty is all beauty, the love cannot be conceived as not being eternal, and where the memories of all past loves dim so precipitately as to almost merge into darkness. We also know *bhava* from our experience of grief which, beginning with a finite loss, irradiates all the world at its height. The world becomes empty, and all that is good is felt to be lost forever. We even know of the quality of *bhava* from states of extreme fear when the smallest sound, the minutest changes of light and shade, the quivering shapes of objects in the dark, all take on an air of extreme menace. The threat becomes eternal, with nary a thought that it might ever end.

Bhava, then, is a way of experiencing which is done "with all one's heart, all one's soul, and all one's might." The *bhava* fills the ecstatic mystic, as it did Ramakrishna, to the brim. He is not depleted, and there is no need for that restitution in delusion and hallucination that is the prime work of insanity. In a *bhava*, Ramakrishna rekindled the world with fresh vision, discovering or rather endowing it with newfound beauty and harmony. *Bhava* animated his relation with nature and human beings, deepened his sensate and metaphysical responsiveness.

Bhava, then, is creative experiencing, or rather the ground for all creativity—mystical, artistic, or scientific. The capacity for *bhava* is what an ideal analysis strives for, an openness toward experiencing, a capacity for 'experiencing experience' as Bion would call it. All the other gains of analysis—insight into one's conflicts, the capacity to experience pleasure without guilt, ability to tolerate anxiety without being crippled, development of a reliable reality testing, and so on —are secondary to the birth of the analytic *bhava*. Of course, the analytic *bhava*, the total openness to the analytic situation manifested in the capacity to really *free*-associate, is not simply a goal to be reached at the end of analysis, but a state to strive for in every session. In the language of the traditional drive-defense analytic model, if we divide defenses into creative and uncreative, the latter by definition pathological, then the capacity for *bhava* is perhaps the most creative of defenses and needs a place of honor beside and even beyond sublimation.

From *bhava*, the ground of mystical creativity, let us turn to *darshan*, vision, the mystic's primary creative product, his particular non-material creation or mystical art. Ramakrishna's explanation of visionary experience is simple, heartfelt, and sensuous. "God cannot be seen with these physical eyes. In the course of spiritual discipline *(sadhana)* one gets a love's body endowed with love eyes, love ears, and so on. One sees God with these love eyes. One hears His voice with these love ears. One even gets a penis and a vagina made of love. With this love body one enjoys intercourse with the soul." [32]

In my own explorations, I prefer to use the religious term vision rather than its psychiatric counterpart hallucination for the same reason that I have talked of mystical *ecstasy* rather than of euphoria, namely the connotations of psychopathology associated with psychiatric categories. The distinction between the two, though, is not very hard and fast, their boundaries constantly shifting. Both can be produced by severe depression or manic excitement, toxic psychosis due to exhaustion or starvation or sensory deprivation or simply a febrile illness. What is important in distinguishing them is their meaning and content and not their origin.

Visions are like hallucinations in that they too are images, such as flashes of light, which are visually perceived without the external stimulation of the organ of sight. They are, however, not hallucinations in that they occur during the course of intense religious experience rather than during a psychotic episode. They are thus less bizarre and less disorganized. Visions belong more to the realm of perceptions that take place, say, during a dream, while falling asleep (hypnagogic) or when awakening (hypnopompic). None of these can be called a consequence of psychic impairment. Visions are, then, special kinds of dreams which find their way into waking life. To have vision is in itself as much a manifestation of mental disorder as is the corresponding process of real events being drawn across the barrier of sleep into the formation of dreams. Freud recognized the special nature of visions when, in an aside on the psychology of the mystic, he remarked, "It is easy to imagine, too, that certain mystics may succeed in upsetting the normal relations between the different regions of the mind, so that, for instance, perception may be able to grasp happenings in the depths of the ego and in the id which were otherwise inaccessible to it."[33]

Ramakrishna's visions, as perhaps those of other mystics, do not constitute a unitary phenomenon. They span the whole range from what can be fairly described as hallucinations in the psychiatric sense, through more or less conscious visions, to what I would call "unconscious visions" (or "visions of the unconscious"?) which cannot be described since the observing ego is absent. These are the ineffable "salt doll" visions which comprise a small, though perhaps the most striking part of the total mystical repertoire.

Before we discuss the various kinds of visions, let us note their central common feature: the intense affect they generate, an affect that endows them with their characteristic sense of noesis. The affect, so strong that it is experienced as *knowing*, partakes of some of the quality of the symbiotic state in infancy when the child knew the mother through an interchange of their feelings, when affect and cognition were not differentiated from one another.[34]

The affects are also manifested in the body, and Ramakrishna's visions had certain well-defined physical correlates. At times, he would shudder while tears of joy streamed unchecked down his cheeks. At other times, his eyes would become half-closed and unfocused, a faint smile playing around the mouth while his body became completely rigid and had to be supported by a disciple lest he fall and hurt himself. The accompaniment to certain other trance states was a flushed chest or a strong burning sensation all over the body. Ramakrishna reports that once when in such a state, Brahmani, his tantric guru, tried to lead him to his bath. She could not hold his hand so hot was his skin, and she had to wrap him in a sheet. The earth that stuck to his body while he was lying on the ground became baked. Then there is the feeling of being famished—one wonders, spiritual receptivity with a bodily analogue (or is it vice versa)? Or there are the bouts of gluttony in which he consumed enormous quantities of food, generally sweets. The craving for a particular dish or a sweet would come upon Ramakrishna unexpectedly, at any time of night or day. At these moments, Ramakrishna would be like a pregnant woman who is dominated by her obsession and cannot rest till the craving is satisfied.

From inside the tradition, all these manifestations are some of the nineteen bodily signs of the mystical experience. To the analyst, however, they are a further confirmation of the mystic's access to a period in early life—"oral" in the classical nomenclature—when the boundary between psyche and soma was much more porous than is the case in adulthood. His is the reclamation of a truly dialogical period wherein engendered affects were discharged through the body while physical experience found easy expression in affective states. Ramakrishna's longing for the Mother, accompanied by breathlessness of a kind where he feels he is about to die, for instance, is akin to a certain type of asthmatic bodily manifestation of a dammed-up urge for the mother's succor.

Coming back to the various types of visions, the hallucinations, unbidden and unwelcome, belong to his period of insanity (*unmada*): "I would spit on the ground when I saw them. But they would follow me and obsess me like ghosts. On the day after such a vision I would have a severe attack of diarrhoea, and all these ecstasies would pass out through my bowels."[35]

These hallucinations, or better, nightmarish visions, are not alien but perhaps as much a part of Ramakrishna's personality as are his artistic sensibility or his more elevated, mystical visions. Their essential linkage may be better understood if we take recourse to Ernst Hartmann's work on nightmares.[36]

In his study of nonpsychiatric volunteers who suffered from nightmares since childhood, Hartmann found that these subjects were usually sensitive people with a strong artistic bent and creative potential. More important, they demonstrate what he calls "thin boundaries of the mind," a permeability between self and object, waking/sleeping, fantasy/reality, adult/child, human/animal, and other such boundaries, which are relatively fixed for most people. The thin boundary of the mind, Hartmann tries to show, is at the root of both their artistic sensibility and potential for nightmares. It is tempting to speculate that Ramakrishna, and perhaps most other mystics, have a genetic biological predisposition, reinforced by some early experiences to which we will come later, to thin boundaries, also between nightmarish and ecstatic visions.

The second class of visions are the conscious ones. Welcomed by a prepared mind, they fall on a receptive ground. Conscious visions may be symbolic representations of an ongoing psychic process, the symbols taken from the mystic's religious and cultural tradition. This is true, for instance, of Ramakrishna's vision of his "enlightenment," which he "saw" in the traditional Yogic imagery of Kundalini, the coiled serpent energy rising through the different centers *(chakras)* of his body and opening up the "lotuses" associated with these centers, a specifically Hindu metaphor for mental transformation and the opening up of the psyche to hitherto inaccessible psychic experience. "I saw a twenty-two, twenty-three-year-old, exactly resembling me, enter the Sushumna nerve and with his tongue "sport" *(raman)* with the vulva-*(yoni)* shaped lotuses. He began with the center at the anus, through the centers of the penis, navel, and so on. The respective four-petaled, six-petaled, and ten-petaled lotuses which had been drooping, rose high and blossomed. I distinctly remember that when he came to the heart and sported with it with his tongue, the twelve-petaled lotus which had been drooping rose high and opened its petals. Then he came to the sixteen-petaled lotus in the throat and the two-petaled one in the forehead. And last of all, the thousand-petaled lotus in the head blossomed."[37] This particular vision, in which self-representation is split into observing and participating aspects, can also be seen through psychiatric glasses as a heutroscopic depersonalization which occurs particularly among individuals with tendencies toward self-contemplation and introspection. Yet in the absence of any associated painful or anxious affect and the fact that this kind of vision was only one among Ramakrishna's vast repertoire of visions with very different structures and qualities, I would tend to see its ground in a creativity, akin to the heightened fantasy of an artist or a writer, rather than in pathology. Goethe and Maupassant are two instances of creative writers who also experienced the phenomenon of their doubles.[38]

Other conscious visions are visual insights, images full of conviction and sudden clarity, couched either in a universal-mystical or in a particular, cultural-historical idiom. Some examples of the former would be seeing the universe filled with sparks of fire, or glittering like a lake of quicksilver, or all its quarters illuminated with the light of myriad candles. Such visions of light, we mentioned earlier, have been reported by mystics throughout the ages, and, indeed, seeing the divine light has been a central feature of many mystical cults, including seventeenth-century Quakerism. Another visual insight of the universal variety is seeing everything throbbing with consciousness: "Sometimes I see the same consciousness playing in small fish that is animating the world. Sometimes I see the world soaked with consciousness in the same way as the earth is soaked with water during the rains."[39]

The full import of the more culturally constituted visions, on the other hand, can only be appreciated if we keep in mind that Ramakrishna was a Hindu Brahmin living at a time—the nineteenth century, and place—rural Bengal—in which the ideas of pollution and polluting substances were strong, caste taboos strict, and the threatened loss of caste a horror of the first magnitude. Visions dissolving religious distinctions and caste taboos, such as the ones on touching forbidden substances or taking foods from forbidden persons, were thus primarily expressed in a cultural imagery relevant to Ramakrishna's community. For instance, "Then I was shown a Muslim with a long beard who came to me with rice in an earthen plate. He fed other Muslims and also gave me some grains to eat. Mother showed me there exists only one and not two."[40] "Another day I saw excrement, urine, rice, vegetables, and other foods. Suddenly the soul came out of my body and, like a flame, touched everything: excrement, urine, everything was tasted. It was revealed that everything is one, that there is no difference." [41] Or, when on the repeated egging on by his nephew, he asked the Goddess for occult powers and saw a middle-aged prostitute come up, squat on her haunches with her back to him, and proceed to evacuate. The vision revealed that occult powers were the shit of that whore.

There is another class of visions, or strictly speaking, mystical illusions, since these rest on a transmutation of external stimuli into creations which are nearer to those of the artist. Thus the way an English boy leans against a tree is transformed into a vision of Krishna; a prostitute walking toward him is changed into a vision of the Mother Goddess—both images irradiate his body and mind with beneficence. In Blake's words, these illusions are "auguries of innocence" enabling the mystic "to see a world in a grain of sand, and a heaven in a wild flower."

And, finally, there are the indescribable, unconscious visions. "You see," Ramakrishna once said to his disciples, "something goes up creeping from the feet to the head. Consciousness continues to exist as long as this power does not reach the head; but as soon as it reaches the head, all consciousness is completely lost. There is no seeing or hearing anymore, much less speaking. Who can speak? The very idea of 'I' and 'You' vanishes. While it (the serpent power) goes up, I feel a desire to tell you everything—how many visions I experience, of their nature, etc. Until it comes to this place (showing the heart) or at most this place (showing the throat) speaking is possible, and I do speak. But the moment it goes up beyond this place (showing the throat) someone forcibly presses the mouth, as it were, and I lose all consciousness. I cannot control it. Suppose I try to describe what kind of visions I experience when it goes beyond this place (showing the throat). As soon as I begin to think of them for the purpose of description, the mind rushes immediately up, and speaking becomes impossible." [42]

His feelings during these visions could then only be expressed in metaphors— "I feel like a fish released from a pot into the water of the Ganges." Ramakrishna, however, does not seem to have been overly enamored of these states which have been so often held as the apex of the mystical experience. He consciously tried to keep a trace of the observing ego—a little spark of the big fire—so as not to completely disappear, or disappear for a long time, into the *unio mystica* with its non differentiation of "I" and the "Other." "In *samadhi*, I lose outer consciousness completely, but God generally keeps a little trace of the ego in me for the enjoyment [here he uses a deliberately sensual metaphor, *vilas*] of intercourse. Enjoyment is only possible when 'I' and 'You' remain." As he maintained, "I want to taste sugar, not become sugar." Yet, in spite of himself, he was often the salt doll that went into the ocean.

The unconscious visions, irreducible to language, are different from other visions which are ineffable only in the sense that their description can never be complete. The unconscious visions are a return to the world before the existence of language, visions of "reality" through the destruction of language that the particular mystical act entails. As Octavio Paz puts it, "Language sinks its roots into this world but transforms its juices and reactions into signs and symbols. Language is the consequence (or the cause) of our exile from the universe, signifying the distance between things and ourselves. If our exile were to come to an end, language would come to an end." [43] The salt doll ends exile, writes a finis to language.

The vicissitudes of separation have been, of course, at the heart of psychoanalytic theorizing on mysticism. The yearning to be reunited with a perfect, omnipotent being, the longing for the blissful soothing and nursing associated with the mother of earliest infancy (perhaps as much an adult myth as an infantile reality), has been consensually deemed the core of mystical motivation. What has been controversial is the way this longing has been viewed and the value placed on it by different analysts.

The traditional view, initiated by Freud, sees this yearning as reactive, a defense against the hatred directed toward the Oedipal father. For writers influenced by Melanie Klein, the longing for the blissful "good" mother is a defensive denial of her terrifying and hated aspects.[44] Given the limitation that Ramakrishna did not spend any time on the couch (but, then, neither have other theorists had mystics as patients), I can only say that there is no evidence in the voluminous record of his conversations, reminiscences, and accounts of his visions which is remotely suggestive of any strong hostility toward the Oedipal father. The evidence for the denial of the dreaded aspects of the mother is slightly greater, namely through a plausible interpretation of some elements of his vision in the Kali temple when he had taken up a sword to kill himself. However, seen in the total context of a large number of visions of the Mother Goddess, the ambiguous evidence of one particular vision is not enough to compel an acceptance of the Kleinian notions on mystical motivation.

Paul Horton has advanced a more adaptive view of mystical yearning and mystical states, especially during adolescence.[45] He sees them as a consequence of the pangs of separation in which the felt reality of being utterly and agonizingly alone is *transiently* denied. The mystical experience is then a transitional phenomenon which soothes and reassures much as a baby is soothed by a blanket, a child by a stuffed toy or fairy tale, an adult by a particular piece of music—all these various creations, material and nonmaterial, providing opportunities for the controlled illusion that heals.

There is much to be said for the hypothesis that experiences of separation and loss spurred Ramakrishna onto the mystical path. We know that Ramakrishna's first quasi-mystical ecstasy when he became unconscious at the sight of white cranes flying against a background of dark clouds took place in the last year of his father's final illness (according to one place in Ramakrishna's reminiscences, two years after his father's death), that is, at a time of an impending loss. And I have described the marked change that came over Ramakrishna—his heightened mystical yearnings with all the outward signs of a full-scale depression—at the death of his brother, at a time in his life cycle, during adolescence, when the developing ego is particularly vulnerable to stress. Here, Ramakrishna is not unlike some of the Christian mystics in whose lives too, as David Aberbach has demonstrated, one could hypothesize a link between personal loss and their mystical calling.[46] Teresa of Avila's life in the church began with the death of her mother when Teresa was twelve years old. The loss of a parent or parent surrogate may also be an early one, heightening a later sense of abandonment and the subsequent search for the "eternal Thou," as perhaps in the examples of St. John of the Cross, whose father died a few months after his birth, or of Martin Buber, whose mother deserted him when he was three.

The mystical path is then also a way of lessening the agony of separation, mitigating the grief at loss, reducing the sadness of bereavement. In my own interviews with members of a mystical cult in India, loss was the single most important factor in their decision to seek its membership. The very embarkation on the mystical path had a therapeutic effect by itself, while any experience of a mystical state had a further marked effect in altering the person's dysphoric state of mind.[47] In contrast to the person's previous feelings of apathy and depression, the turn to mysticism had the consequence of his dealing with grief in a more orderly and more detached, though in a more transcendent, manner. Perhaps T.S. Eliot is correct in observing that "A man does not join himself with the universe so long as he has anything else to join himself with." [48]

Of course, Ramakrishna's two actual experiences of loss are not sufficient to explain the totality of his mysticism, the intensity of his yearning throughout life to end the state of separation from the Divine, and the acuteness of his distress at the absence of the Mother. The motivational skein of mysticism, as of any other psychic phenomenon, is composed of many strands. One could speculate that the advanced age of his mother at his birth, his family's poverty and thus his mother's added preoccupations with household tasks, the birth of another sibling when he was four, may have led to the emotional unavailability of the mother at a phase of the child's development when his own needs were driving him closer to her. In other words, the suggestion is that in the crucial "rapprochement" phase (which occurs later in India than in psychoanalyst Margaret Mahler's timetable), the mother was unavailable at a time when his anxiety about separation, and its convergent depression, were at their apex. This would fix separation and its associated anxiety as the dominant theme of his inner life. Each feared or actual loss would reactivate separation anxiety together with a concomitant effort at combating it by reclaiming in fantasy an adored and adoring intimacy with the maternal matrix. The unity Ramakrishna aimed for is, then, not the mergerlike states of the infant at the breast, though these too prefigured his trances, but the ending of separation striven for by the toddler. It is a state in which both mother and child have boundaries in relation to each other while another boundary encloses their "double unit" from the rest of the world. Here the enjoyment of the mother's presence is deeply sensuous, almost ecstatic, and informs Ramakrishna's selection of words, images and metaphors that describe his experiences.

Together with the speculated impact of early mother-child interaction in Ramakrishna's psychic life, admittedly a construct derived from analytic theory rather than a reconstruction based on compelling psychobiographical evidence, I would tend to attribute his acute sensitivity to the theme of separation to the mystical gift (or curse) of a specific kind of creative experiencing. This can be understood more clearly, if we take recourse to some ideas of the "metaphysical" analysts mentioned earlier.

Lacan, for instance, has postulated that man's psychic life constantly seeks to deal with a primordial state of affairs which he calls The Real. The Real itself is unknowable, though we constantly create myths as its markers. Perhaps the principal myth involves the rupture of a basic union, the separation from the mother's body, leaving us with a fundamental feeling of incompletion. The fantasies around this insufficiency are universal, governing the psyche of both patients and analysts alike. In the psyche, this lack is translated as desire, and the human venture is a history of desire as it ceaselessly loses and discovers itself in (what Lacan calls) The Imaginary and, with the advent of language, The Symbolic order. Born of rupture, desire's fate is an endless quest for the lost object; all real objects merely interrupt the search. As the Barandes put it, "It is the task of the *neotenique* [i.e., immature, even fetalized being] being separated from its original union by its fall into life and into time, to invent detours for itself, deviations of object as well as means and aims. Its condition is inexorably perverse—if perversions must be."[49] The mystical quest seeks to rescue from primal repression the constantly lived contrast between an original interlocking and a radical rupture. The mystic, unlike most others, does not mistake his hunger for its fulfillment. If we are all fundamentally perverse in the play of our desire, then the mystic is the only one who seeks to go beyond the illusion of The Imaginary and, yes, also the *maya* of The Symbolic register.

One of Ramakrishna's more "private" visions attempts to paint the issue of separation with crude yet compelling brushstrokes. As Bion would say, here he is like the analyst who knows that emotional truth is ineffable, available only in intimations and approximations. Like the Bionian analyst, the mystic too is compelled to use terms from sensuous experience to point to a realm beyond this experience. "Let me tell you a very secret experience. Sitting in a pine grove, I had the vision of a small, hidden [literally "thief's door"] entrance to a room. I could not see what was inside the room. I tried to bore a hole with a nail file but did not succeed. As I bored the hole it would fill up again and again. And then suddenly I made a big opening." He kept quiet and then started speaking again. "These are all higher matters. I feel someone is closing my mouth. I have seen God residing in the vagina. I saw Him there at the time of sexual intercourse of a dog and a bitch."[50]

Ramakrishna's vision, followed by an associative sequel, does not need extended analytic gloss. The small secret opening to a room into which he cannot see and which he tries to keep open, the seeing of God in the genitals of a bitch in intercourse, do not encode the mystical preoccupation with opening a way back to the self-other interlocking in any complex symbolic language. This interlocking, the mystical unity, is not unitary. As we saw in Ramakrishna's case, it extends in a continuum from the fetalized being's never having known separation from the mother's insides, an expulsion from her womb, through the satiated infant's flowing feelings of merger at the breast, to the toddler being pulled back to the mother as if held at one end of an invisible string.

What I am emphasizing, however, is not the traditional analytic agenda of pathological, defensive, or compensatory uses of these various degrees of dyadic unity in mystical experiencing. As Michael Eigen has elaborated in a series of papers, for Freud, ideal experiencing, that is, states or moments of beatific (or horrific) perfection, in which I would include the mystical states, usually involved something in disguise—mother, father, sex, aggression and so on.[51] Lacan, Winnicott and Bion (and implicitly also Erikson), on the other hand, look at ideal experiencing in its own right, as a spontaneously unfolding capacity for creative experiencing. This capacity can be deployed defensively as has been spelled out in detail in the Freudian literature, but it is not coterminous with defense.

All these authors emphasize the positive, regenerative aspects of this experiencing not as idealists but as empirical analysts who chart out its developmental vicissitudes from early infancy onward. The experiencing itself, they maintain, should not be confused with the introjection of the mother and father images or functions. These only foster or hamper this capacity. "If one reads these authors carefully, one discovers that *the primary object of creative experiencing is not mother or father but the unknowable ground of creativeness as such.* Winnicott, for example, emphasizes that what is at stake in transitional experiencing is not mainly a self or object (mother) substitute, but the creation of a symbol, of symbolizing experiencing itself. The subject lives through and toward creative immersion (including phases of chaos, unintegration, waiting)."[52] What we should then pay equal attention to is not only the conflicts of the mystic that threaten to deform or disperse his creative experiencing, but the experiencing itself—its content, context, and evolution.

Most of us harbor tantalizing "forgotten" traces of this kind of experiencing, an apperception where what is happening outside is felt to be the creative act of the original artist (or mystic) within each of us and recognized as such with (in Blake's word) *delight.* For in late infancy and early childhood we did not always see the world as something outside ourselves, to be recognized in detail, adapted, complied with, and fitted into our idiosyncratic inner world, but often as an infinite succession of creative acts.

Mystical experience, then, is one and—in some cultures and at certain historical periods—the preeminent way of uncovering the vein of creativity that runs deep in all of us. For some, it is the throes of romantic love that gives inklings of our original freshness of vision.

Others may strive for creative experiencing in art or in natural science. In the West, the similarities between mystics and creative artists and scientists have been pointed out since the beginning of the century. Evelyn Underhill in her path-breaking work on mysticism emphasized the resemblance between artistic geniuses and mystics— though one should hesitate to use the terms as interchangeable —while James Leuba pointed out the similarity at a more mundane level in creative phenomena of the daily kind and at a lower level of intensity.[53] In China, we know that it was the mystical Taoists stressing spontaneity, "inaction," "emptying the mind," rather than the rational Confucians, who stimulated Chinese scientific discovery. In India, too, in different epochs, the striving for mystical experience through art, especially music, has been a commonly accepted and time-honored practice. And Albert Einstein writes of his own motivations for the scientific enterprise, "The most beautiful, the most profound emotion we can experience is the sensation of the mystical. It is the fundamental emotion that stands at the cradle of true art and science." Einstein goes on to say that there is a need "to escape from everyday life with its painful crudity and hopeless dreariness, from fetters of one's own shifting desires." Instead the scientist and the artist creates his own reality, substituting it for the world of experience and thus overcoming it: "Each makes his own cosmos and its construction the pivot of his emotional life, in order to find in this way peace and security which he cannot find in the narrow whirlpool of personal experience." [54] Here it seems to me that Einstein is not talking as someone who is depressed but with a creative individual's clear-sighted and inevitable response to the world as it is. When Buddha, as the young Siddhartha confronted with illness, old-age, and death proclaims "*Sabbam dukham*" (All is suffering), he too is not depressed but in perfect attunement with the reality principle. To see the world with a creative eye but a sober perspective is perhaps our greatest adaptation to reality—a state where Buddha, Freud and Ramakrishna come together.

Sexuality and the Mystical Experience

Ramakrishna was one with other Vaishnava mystics in his insistence that sexuality, by which he meant male sexuality, phallic desire, constituted the biggest obstacle to mystical experiencing. This is a formulation with which psychoanalysts will not have any quarrel. For both male and female infants, the differentiation between self and object is achieved and ego boundaries constituted by a gradual detachment from the mother. The presence of the father is vital for this process. Whereas the masculinity of the father makes it possible for the boy to overcome his primary femininity, the presence of the paternal phallus also helps to protect the little girl from fusional tendencies with the mother. Male sexuality and male desire may thus be viewed as obstacles in the path of fusion, the phallus as the prime symbol of boundaries the mystic seeks to transcend.

The renunciation of adult masculinity is not only a feature of Hindu devotional mysticism but is also a feature of Christian emotional mysticism of medieval and early modern Europe. Affective prayer or Bernardine mysticism, as it has often been called after the influential sermons of the eleventh-century saint Bernard of Clairvaux, possesses a striking affinity to its Hindu counterpart. Femininity pervades both. In the case of medieval Europe, most of the practicing mystics were women. But even the outstanding male mystics—St. John of the Cross, Francois de Sales, Fenelon—show strong feminine identifications and produced their most important ideas under the direct influence of women.[55] The psychological stance of Christian ecstatics toward

Divinity, paralleling that of the Vaishnava mystics, is either that of the infant toward a loving maternal parent, or of a woman toward a youthful lover. Like the Hindus, the Christian mystics too disavowed or overthrew the paternal phallus as they divested the Judeo-Christian God of much of his original masculinity and sternness, virtually relegating him to the role of a grandfather. The message of the European emotional mystics seems to be the same as that of Ramakrishna: the actual gender of the mystic is not important for his practice. It is, however, vital that the mystic accept and cultivate his or her femininity to the point that the female-self part becomes dominant in his or her inner psychic reality.

Of the many mystical disciplines, the one Ramakrishna could never practice was the " heroic" one of Tantra where, at its culmination, God as a female is sought to be pleased—or perhaps I should say, pleasured—as a man pleases a woman through intercourse. In his own tantric training, he had escaped the demand for ritual sex by going into an ecstatic state just before he had to actually "perform". He repeatedly warned his disciples against *kamini-kanchani* (literally, woman and gold), and his advice to novices on the mystical path was to avoid the female sex altogether, the whirlpool in which even Brahma and Vishnu struggle for their lives. For a renunciant, he felt, to sit with a woman or talk to her for a long time was a kind of sexual intercourse of which there were eight kinds. Some of these were to listen to a woman, to talk to her in secret, to keep and enjoy something belonging to a woman, to touch her, and so on. Given the fact that a vast majority of widely known mystics, at least in medieval Christian and devotional Hindu traditions, have been celibates, one wonders whether celibacy, with its profound influence on hormonal balance, is not an important physiological technique for mystical ecstasy.

The prescribed avoidance of women was only for beginners. Once mystical knowledge was gained, sexual differentiation too vanished: "Then you don't have much to fear. After reaching the roof you can dance as much as you like, but not on the stairs." Yet though Ramakrishna constantly reiterated that he looked at the breasts of every woman as those of his mother, that he felt as a child or as another woman with women, his male awareness of women as sexual beings, and of the dangers of a desire that separates and bifurcates, never quite disappeared as his biographers would have us believe. He felt uncomfortable with female devotees sitting in his room and would ask them to go and visit the temple as soon as he could decently get rid of them. Being touched by a woman was not a matter of unconcern but evoked strong physical reactions. "If a woman touches me, I fall ill. That part of my body aches as if stung by a horned fish. If I touch a woman my hand becomes numb; it aches. If in a friendly spirit I approach a woman and begin to talk to her, I feel as if a curtain has come down between us." [56] However minimal his sexual conflict, even a great mystic seems to retain at least a vestigial entanglement with the world of desire. In his normal nonecstatic state, Ramakrishna too was never quite free of the sexual *maya*, free from the delight, wisdom, beauty, and pain of the "illusion" which so beguiles the rest of us.

Ramakrishna's attempted renunciation of male sexual desire is the subject of one vision, although as someone who claimed to never having even dreamt of intercourse with a woman, the *conscious* promptings of desire could not have been too peremptory. "During the *sadhanas*, I vividly perceived a heap of rupees, a shawl, a plate of sweets and two women. 'Do you want to enjoy any of these things?' I asked my mind. 'No,' replied the mind. I saw the insides of those women, of what is in them; entrails, piss, shit, phlegm and such things." [57] We can, of course, try to understand the contents of this vision in biographical terms. Money, shawl, and sweets embody over-powering temptations for a boy who grew up in a poor family whose dire financial straits allowed but the most spartan of fares. Similarly, one possible cause for the hankering after sexual purity in his youth could be a deep feeling of shame he associated with the sexual act. In a country and at a time where women not infrequently became grand-mothers in their late twenties, where sexual activity has always been considered a prerogative of the young—sexual desire of older men and women occasioning derisive laughter—Ramakrishna's birth itself (followed by that of the sister) is the sign of a tainted and deeply mortifying sexuality of his old parents. We have already seen how Ramakrishna's enduring wish to be a woman, expressed variously in dressing and moving his limbs like one, his fantasy of being a girl widow who secretly trysts with Krishna every evening, fitted in well with a tenet of Vaishnava mysticism that all mankind is female while God alone is male. Ramakrishna would approvingly cite the opinion that irrespective of biological gender everyone with nipples is a female. Arjuna, the heroic warrior of the Mahabharata, and Krishna are the only exceptional males since they do not have nipples. In the *madhurya bhava*, Ramakrishna had even tried to engender in himself female erotic feelings. Moved by an intense love for Krishna, "such as a woman feels for her lover," he had stretched out his arms to embrace the Lord's stone idols.

Just as the writings of medieval European female mystics, wherein they wax rhapsodic over their ecstatic union with Jesus, portrayed as an exceedingly handsome and loving bridegroom of the human soul, have been analyzed as expressions of a pathological, hysterical sexuality, it would not be difficult to diagnose Ramakrishna in traditional Freudian terms as a secondary transsexual. He would seamlessly fit in with Robert Stoller's description of the secondary transsexual as being someone who differs from his primary counterpart in that he does not appear feminine from the start of any behavior that may be classed in gender terms.[58] Under the surface of masculinity, however, there is the persistent impulse toward being feminine, an urge which generally manifests itself in adolescence. The most obvious manifestation of these urges is the wish or the actual wearing of women's clothes. Though these urges may gather in strength and last for longer and longer periods, the masculine aspects of identity are never completely submerged.

Ramakrishna's open espousal and expression of his feminine identifications as a boy, however, also have to do with the greater tolerance of his community and its culture towards such identifications. His urge toward femininity did not meet an unyielding opposition or strenuous attempts at suppression by an enforced participation in masculine play. Any transsexual or homosexual labels may obscure his sense of comfort and easy familiarity with the feminine components of his self. It may hide the fact that the freeing of femininity from repression or disavowal in man and *vice versa* in a woman may be a great human achievement rather than an illness or a deviation. The deviation may actually lie, as in one view of the etiology of homosexuality, in the *inability* to come to terms with the opposite sexual personality in one's self.[59]

Summarizing, I would say that the male-self part of Ramakrishna's personality was split off in early childhood and tended to grow, if at all, rather slowly. In contrast, the female-self part of his personality dominated his inner psychic reality. Ramakrishna's girl-self was neither repressed nor disassociated but could mature to an extent where psychically he could even possess female sexual equipment and enjoy female sexual experience.

Yet even a celebratory avowal of secondary femininity in a male mystic may not be enough to exhaust the mystery of the link between sexuality and mysticism. For if, together with "infant-likeness," secondary femininity and female bodily experience—breastpride, absence of male external genitalia, the presence of vulva and womb—are important for affective mysticism, then women will be seen as having a head start in this particular human enterprise. They naturally are what a male aspirant must become. This may be true though it has yet to be demonstrated that gender makes a substantial difference in the making of a mystic. What is perhaps essential in mysticism is not the presence of secondary but of "primary" femininity—the "pure female element" (not the female person) in Winnicott's sense of the term. In his theory of the life of male and female elements in a person, the purely male element, in both man and woman, presupposes separateness and traffics in terms of active relating, or being passively related to, and is backed by the whole apparatus of instinctual drives.[60] The female element, on the other hand, relates to the other—the breast, the mother (both with a small and capital "m")—in the sense of an identity between the two. When this element finds the other, it is the self that has been found. It is the female element that establishes the simplest, the most primary of experiences, the experience of *being*. Winnicott remarks, "Psychoanalysts have perhaps given special attention to this male element or drive aspect of object relating and yet have neglected the subject-object identity to which I am drawing attention here, which is at the basis of the capacity to be. The male element *does* (active-passive) while the female element *is* (in males and females) and concludes "After being—doing and being done to. But first *being*."[61]

Looking at Ramakrishna's sexuality in relation to his mystical experience in terms of oral, anal, and phallic stages of development or of identifications with mother, father and so on, as in classical analytic discourse, is then to forget that this discourse itself may be based on the life of the male element. Our psychology has still little to say of the distilled female element, the primary femininity, at the heart of emotional mysticism. The pure female element, in both men and women, continues to testify to the category of mystery as a basic dimension in which we all, and especially the mystic, live. As analysts, however, we cannot look at mystery as something eternally beyond human comprehension, but as a phenomenon to which we repeatedly return to increase our understanding. As our perspectives change, our earlier views do not get replaced but are subsumed in an ever-widening set of meanings.

2
The Guru as Healer

The contemporary images of the Indian guru, the sacred center of Hindu religious and philosophical traditions, are many. He is that stately figure in spotless white or saffron robes, with flowing locks and beard, to all appearances the younger brother of a brown Jehovah. To be approached in awe and reverence, he is someone who makes possible the disciple's fateful encounter with the mystery lying at the heart of human life. He is also the Rasputin look-alike, with piercing yet warm eyes, hypnotic and seductive at once, a promiser of secret ecstasies and radical transformations of consciousness and life. The guru is also the venerable guardian of ancient, esoteric traditions, benevolently watchful over the disciple's experiences in faith, gently facilitating his sense of identity and self. He can also be (to use the imagery of Pupul Jayakar, the biographer of the Indian sage Jiddu Krishnamurti), "the silent, straight-backed stranger, the mendicant who stands waiting at the doorways of home and mind, holding an invitation to otherness," evoking "passionate longings, anguish and a reaching out physically and inwardly to that which is unattainable."[1]

In the above snapshots we find little trace of the old polarity which characterized the guru image. This polarity consisted of the worldly, orthodox teacher guru at one end representing relative, empirical knowledge, and the otherworldly, mystic guru at the other pole who was the representative of esoteric, existential knowledge. In Hindu terms, the dominant image of the guru seems to have decisively shifted toward the *moksha* (liberation) guru rather than the *dharma* (virtue) guru, toward the *bhakti* (devotional) guru rather than the *jnana* (knowledge) guru or, in tantric terms, toward the *diksha* (initiation) guru who initiated the novice into methods of salvation rather than the *shiksha* (teaching) guru who taught the scriptures and explained the meaning and purpose of life.[2]

This was, of course, not always the case. In Vedic times (1500–500 B.C.), when man's encounter with the sacred mysteries took place through ritual, the guru was more a guide to their correct performance and an instructor in religious duties. A teacher deserving respect and a measure of obedience, he was not yet a mysterious figure of awe and the venerated incarnation of divinity.

In the later Upanishadic era (800–500 B.C.), the polar shift begins in earnest as the person of the guru starts to replace Vedic rituals as the path to spiritual liberation. He now changes from a knower and dweller in Brahman to being the only conduit to Brahman. Yet the Upanishadic guru is still recognizably human—a teacher of acute intellect, astute and compassionate, demanding from the disciple the exercise of his reason rather than exercises in submission and blind obedience. When, in the seventh-century A.D., the great Shankara, in his project of reviving the ancient Brahminical tradition, seeks to resurrect the Upanishadic guru, he sees in him a teacher who "is calm, tranquil, childlike, silent and free from distracting motivations. Although learned he should be as a child, parading neither wisdom, nor learning, nor virtue itself. . . . He is a reservoir of mercy who teaches out of compassion to the multitude. He is sympathetic to the conditions of the student and is able to act with empathy towards him."[3] In the disciple's spiritual quest, Shankara's guru places reason on par with scriptural authority and constantly exhorts the student to test and verify the teachings through his own experience. Every student needs to discover anew for himself or herself what is already known, a spiritual patrimony which has to be earned each time for it to become truly one's own. Here, the ideal of the Hindu guru was not too far removed from the Buddhist master who, too, constructed experience-near situations to illustrate a teaching and who saw the master-disciple relationship as one of perfect equality in self-realization, with radical insight as its goal. The relationship between the guru and disciple was of intimacy, not of merger. Both the guru and disciple were separate individuals, and potential equals, though striving for ever-greater closeness.

From the seventh-century onwards, the swing away from the teacher image of the guru received its greatest momentum with the rise of the *bhakti* cults in both North and South India. Devotional surrender on the part of the disciple, with such features as ritualistic service to the guru, the worship of his feet, bodily prostration and other forms of veneration, and divine grace (*prasada*) on the part of the guru, mark the guru-disciple relationship. "Guru and Govind [i.e., Lord Krishna] stand before me," says the fifteenth-century saint-poet Kabir, and asks, "Whose feet should I touch?" The answer is, "The guru gets the offering. He shows the way to Govind."[4] The operative word is now love rather than understanding. To quote Kabir again:

> Reading book after book, the whole world died
> And none ever became learned
> He who can decipher just a syllable of "love"
> is the true learned man (pandit)[5]

With the spread of tantric cults around 1000 A.D., the guru not only shows the way to the Lord, but is the Lord. "There is no higher god than guru," tantric texts tell us, "No higher truth than the guru." "The guru is father, the guru is mother, the guru is the God Shiva. When Shiva is angry, the guru is the Savior. But when the guru is angry, there is no one who can save you."[6] The guru is now an extraordinary figure of divine mystery and power, greater than the scriptures and the gods, and all that the disciple requires to realize his own godlike nature, his extraordinary identity as Lawrence Babb puts it, is to merge his substantial and spiritual being with that of the guru.[7] The ambiguities of thought and the agonizings of reason can be safely sidestepped since the way is no longer through Upanishadic listening, reflection, and concentration but through a complete and willful surrender—the offering of *tana, mana*, and *dhana* (body, mind, and wealth) in the well-known phrase of North Indian devotionalism. The responsibility for the disciple's inner transformation is no longer that of the disciple but of the guru. "One single word of the guru gives liberation," says a tantric text. "All the sciences are masquerades. Only the knowledge flowing out of the guru's mouth is living. All other kinds of knowledge are powerless and cause of suffering."[8]

The combined forces of the *bhakti* and *tantra* pushed toward an ever-increasing deification of the guru, a massive idealization of his mystery and power. The thirteenth-century Marathi saint Jnaneshvara writes of the guru:

> As for his powers,
> He surpasses even the greatness of Shiva,
> With his help,
> The soul attains the state of Brahman;
> But if he is indifferent,
> Brahman has no more worth than a blade of grass.[9]

Complementary to the movement of the guru from man to god is the shift in the disciple from man to child. The favored, the ideal disciple is pure of heart, malleable of character, and a natural renouncer of all adult categories, especially of rational inquiry and of the sexual gift. These images of the guru and disciple and their ideal relationship pervades the Hindu psyche to a substantial extent even today. "Guru is Brahma, guru is Vishnu, guru is Maheshwara," is a verse not only familiar to most Hindus but one that evokes complex cultural longings, that resonates with what is felt to be the best part of their selves and of the Hindu tradition.

Let me not give the impression that the triumphant procession of the liberation/salvation guru in Hindu tradition has gone completely unchallenged. In traditional texts there are at least two instances questioning the need for a guru, admittedly an insignificant number compared to hundreds of tales, parables, and pronouncements extolling him. The first one is from the Uddhavagita in the sixth-century text of Bhagvata Purana where Dattareya, on asked to account for his self-possession and equanimity, lists elements of nature, the river, certain animals, and even a prostitute (from whom he learned autonomy from the sensual world) as his twenty-four gurus. The parable of Dattareya ends with the exhortation, "Learn, above all, from the rhythms of your own body." The second incident is an episode from the Yogavasistha, a text composed between the ninth and twelfth-centuries in Kashmir, wherein Princess Cudala, setting out on her inner journey of self-exploration, deliberately eschews all gurus and external authorities, and reaches her goal through a seven-stage self-analysis.

In more recent times, beginning in the nineteenth-century, there have been reformers who have sought to revive Vedic rituals and Upanishadic religion. They would at the most sanction the teacher guru, such as the socially engaged intellectual swami of the Ramakrishna Mission or of the nineteenth-century reformist movement, Arya Samaj. There have been also reluctant gurus, such as Krishnamurti, who vehemently denied the need for a guru and in fact saw in him the chief obstacle to spiritual liberation. For him and some modern educated Indians the guru institution as it exists today is a focus of all the anti-intellectual and authoritarian tendencies in Hindu society.[10] Yet for the great mass of Hindus, the mystical, charismatic, divine guru image continues to be a beacon of their inner worlds. The allpervasiveness of this image is due to more complex reasons than the mere victory of irrationality over reason, servility over autonomy, or of a contemporary dark age over an earlier golden era.

What I am suggesting here is that the shift from the teacher to the master image is inevitable given the fact that perhaps a major, if not the most significant, role of the guru is that of a healer of emotional suffering and its somatic manifestations. This psychotherapeutic function, insufficiently acknowledged, is clearly visible in well-known modern gurus whose fame depends on their reported healing capabilities, rather than deriving from any mastery of traditional scriptures, philosophical knowledge, of even great spiritual attainments. Of course, in cases of international gurus, the healing is tailored to culture-specific needs. In India there will be more miracles and magical healing, while in the West there will be a greater use of psycho-religious methods and techniques which are not unfamiliar to a psychotherapeutically informed population.[11]

The importance of the healing guru comes through clearly in all available accounts. Ramakrishna's disciple-biographer writes:

> The spiritual teacher has been described in the Guru-gita and other books as the "physician of the world-disease." We did not at all understand that so much hidden meaning was there in it before we had the blessing of meeting the master. We had no notion of the fact that the Guru was indeed the physician of mental diseases and could diagnose at first sight the modifications of the human mind due to influence of spiritual emotions.[12]

Perhaps the most vivid recent account of the therapeutic encounter between a guru and a disciple is contained in Pupul Jayakar's moving description of her first one-to-one meeting with Krishnamurti. The narration could very well also have been of an initial interview with a good analyst. In her early thirties, outwardly active and successful, yet with intimations of something seriously wrong with her life, Jayakar is apprehensive and tries to prepare for the meeting. She begins the interview by talking of the fullness of her life and work, her concern for the underprivileged, her interest in art, her desire to enter politics. As the first flow of words peters out, Jayakar gradually falls silent. "I looked up and saw he was gazing at me; there was a questioning in his eyes and a deep probing. After a pause he said, 'I have noticed you at the discussions. When you are in repose, there is a great sadness on your face.'

"I forgot what I had intended to say, forgot everything but the sorrow within me. I had refused to allow the pain to come through. So deep was it buried that it rarely impinged on my conscious mind. I was horrified of the idea that others would show me pity and sympathy, and had covered up my sorrow with layers of aggression. I had never spoken of this to anyone—not even to myself had I acknowledged my loneliness; but before this silent stranger all masks were swept away. I looked into his eyes and it was my own face I saw reflected. Like a torrent long held in check, the words came."[13]

Jayakar talks of her childhood, of a sensitive lonely girl, "dark of complexion in a family where everyone was fair, unnoticed, a girl when I should have been a boy." She talks of her pregnancies, in one case the baby dying in the womb, in other the birth of a deformed child, a girl who dies in childhood. She tells Krishnamurti of the racking pain of her beloved father's death and the tearing, unendurable agony she feels as she talks. "In his presence the past, hidden in the darkness of the long forgotten, found form and awakened. He was as a mirror that reflected. There was an absence of personality, of the evaluator, to weigh and distort. I kept trying to keep back something of my past but he would not let me. He said, I can see if you want me to. And so the words which for years had been destroying me were said."[14]

Krishnamurti is one of the most "intellectual" of modern gurus, with a following chiefly among the most modern and highly educated sections of Indian society. It is nonetheless the news of his "miracle" cures—deafness in one instance, an acute depression in another—which spreads like wildfire through the *ashrams* all over the country. Crowds of potential disciples gather at his talks, striving to touch his hand, to share in his benediction. "These incidents and the vastness of his silent presence impressed people tremendously," Jayakar writes somewhat ruefully. "The teaching, though they all agreed it was grounded in a total nonduality, appeared too distant and too unattainable."[15]

In my own work with gurus and disciples, I found that many of the latter shared a common pattern in their lives that had led them to a search for the guru and to initiation in his cult.[16] Almost invariably the individual had gone through one or more experiences that had severely mauled his sense of self-worth, if not shattered it completely. In contrast to the rest of us, who must also deal with the painful feelings aroused by temporary depletions in self-esteem, it seems that those who went to gurus grappled with these feelings for a much longer time, sometimes for many years, without being able to change them appreciably. Unable to rid themselves of the feelings of "I have lost everything and the world is empty," or "I have lost everything because I do not deserve anything," they had been on the lookout for someone, somewhere, to restore the lost sense of self-worth and to counteract their hidden image of a failing, depleted self—a search nonetheless desperate for its being mostly unconscious. This "someone" eventually turned out to be the particular guru to whom the seekers were led by events—such as his vision—which in retrospect seemed miraculous.

The conviction and the sense of a miracle having taken place, though projected to the circumstances that led to the individual's initiation into the cult, actually derived from the "miraculous" ending of a persistent and painful internal state, the disappearance of the black depressive cloud that had seemed to be a permanent feature of the individual's life. Perhaps a vignette from a life history will illustrate this pattern more concretely.

Harnam was the youngest of four sons of a peasant family from a North Indian village who had tilled their own land for many generations. As the "baby" of the family, Harnam had been much indulged during his childhood, especially by his mother. She had died when he was eighteen, and ever since her death, he said, a peculiar *udasinta* (sadness) had taken possession of his soul. Though he had all the comforts at home, enough to eat and drink, and an abundant measure of affection from his father and elder brothers, the *udasinta* had persisted. For fifteen long years he said, his soul remained restless, yearning for an unattainable peace. His thoughts often dwelt upon death, of which he developed an exaggerated fear, and he was subject to crippling headaches that confined him to the darkness of his room for long periods. Then, suddenly he had a vision in a dream of the guru (he had seen his photograph earlier), who told him to come to his *ashram* to take initiation into the cult. He had done so; his sadness had disappeared as did his fear and headaches, and he felt the loving omnipresence of the guru as a protection against their return.

Besides cultural encouragement and individual needs, I believe there are some shared developmental experiences of many upper caste Hindu men which contribute to the intensification of the fantasy of guru as healer. In an earlier work, I have described the male child's experience of "second birth," a more or less sudden loss of a relationship of symbiotic intimacy with the mother in late childhood and an entry into the more businesslike relationships of the world of men.[17] Two of the consequences of the "second birth" in the identity development of Hindu men are first, an unconscious tendency to "submit" to an idealized omnipotent figure, both in the inner world of fantasy and in the outside world of making a living, and second the lifelong search for someone, a charismatic leader or a guru, who will provide mentorship and a guiding worldview, thereby restoring intimacy and authority to individual life. I would interpret the same phenomena more explicitly in terms of self psychology. Since I believe some of the concepts of self psychology to be of value in illuminating the healing process in the guru-disciple relationship, these concepts may first need a brief elucidation.

The major focus of the Kohutian psychology of the self is what he called a selfobject.[18] One exists as a person, a self, because a significant other, the selfobject, has addressed one as a self and evoked the self experience. Selfobjects, strictly speaking, are not persons but the subjective aspect of a function performed by a relationship. It is thus more apt to speak of selfobject experiences, intrapsychic rather than interpersonal, which evoke, maintain, and give cohesion to the self.[19] The very emergence and maintenance of the self as a psychological structure, then, depends on the continued presence of an evoking-sustaining-responding matrix of selfobject experiences. Always needed, from birth to death, the absence of these experiences leads to a sense of fragmentation of the self, including, in extreme states of narcissistic starvation, the terrors of self dissolution.

The mode of needed selfobject experiences, of course, changes with age from the simple to the more complex. In a child, the required selfobject experience occurs primarily, though not exclusively (remember the importance of the glow in the mother's eye and of the affirmative timbre in her voice), through physical ministrations. In the adult, symbolic selfobject experiences supplied by his culture, such as religious, aesthetic, and group experiences, may replace some of the more concrete modes of infancy and childhood. In the language of self psychology, the guru is the primary cultural selfobject experience for adults in Hindu tradition and society. For everyone whose self was weakened because of faulty selfobject relations during crucial developmental phases or for those who have been forced into defensive postures by the self's fragility where they are cut off from all normal sustaining and healing selfobject responses, the guru is the culture's irresistible offer for the redressal of injury and the provision of selfobject experience needed for the strengthening of the self.

It is the immanence of the healing moment in the guru-disciple relationship which inevitably pushes the guru image toward that of a divine parent and of the disciple toward that of a small child. Western psychiatrists have tended to focus more on the pathology and the malevolent regression unleashed by the psychic shifts in the images of the self and the guru when therapeutic expectations of the disciples take firm hold.[20] They have talked of the extreme submissiveness of the disciples, of a denial of strong unconscious hostility, of the devotee's deepest desire being of oral dependence on the mother, and so on.

I believe the Western psychiatric emphasis on the pathological and regressive—"bad" regressive—aspects of the guru-disciple relationship does it injustice. However one may prefer the Enlightenment virtues of reason and ideological egalitarianism, the universal power exercised by what I would call the guru fantasy is not to be denied. By guru fantasy I mean the existence of someone, somewhere, who will heal the wounds suffered in the original parent-child relationship. It is the unconscious longing for the curer of the "world-disease," a longing which marks all potentially healing encounters whether they are or not officially termed as such. This fantasy invariably exerts its power in changing the self-image of the seeker and of the healing Other in the directions I have described above.

My own profession, psychoanalysis, in its theories of cure has not escaped from the ubiquitous power of this fantasy. Patients, of course, have always approached analysis and analysts with a full-blown guru fantasy. Analysts, on the other hand, tended at first to believe with Freud that healing took place through knowledge and an expansion of conscious awareness. Yet beginning with one of the most original of the first generation of analysts, Sandor Ferenzci, there has been a growing body of opinion which holds the person of the analyst and his interaction with the patient, in which the analyst counteracts the specific pathogenic deficit of the parent-child relationship, as the prime carriers of the healing moment. Franz Alexander was perhaps the most outright advocate of the analyst adopting corrective postures, but the stress on the role of the analyst as someone who makes up in some fashion or other for a deficient nonempathic parent is met with again and again in analytical literature, especially in the school of object relations. Winnicott, for instance, believed that with patients who suffered from not-good-enough early maternal environment, the analytic setting and the analyst, more than his interpretations, provided an opportunity for the development of an ego, for its integration from ego nuclei. Kohut's self psychology with its stress on the curative powers of the analyst's empathy moves further in the same direction. As Ernst Wolf states the self psychological position, "It is not the content of the information conveyed to the patient, not the substance of the interpretations and interventions made, not the correctness of the therapist's conjectures, not even the therapist's compliance with demands to "mirror" the patient or to be his or her ideal that is pivotal: It is decisive for the progress of the therapeutic endeavor that the patient experience an ambience in which he or she feels respected, accepted and at least a little understood. . . . The person who is the therapist then becomes as crucial a variable as the person who is the patient.[21]

Many years earlier, Sacha Nacht had captured this shift in the psychoanalytic view of healing when he said "it is of more value from the curative point of view, to have a mediocre interpretation supported by good transference than the reverse."[22] In interviews with devotees, the unconscious expectation that the guru will counteract specific parental deficits becomes manifest in the way an individual selects a particular guru. It seems to be a fact that often the Master who is experienced as an incarnation of the Divine by his own disciples leaves other seekers cold. In the politics of gurudom, reverence and worship by your own devotees does not ensure that you are not a figure of indifference, even of derision and contempt, to other gurus and members of *their* cults. Let me illustrate.

Amita, a thirty-year-old woman who is a lecturer in Hindi in a local college, is one of the closest disciples of a contemporary female guru, Nirmala Devi. Born into an orthodox middle-class Brahmin family, she has been engaged in the "search" ever since childhood. "My mother used to worship five hundred and sixty million gods every day," she says in a bitter, contemptuous voice, "but it didn't change her a bit. She was a hot-tempered, dried-up woman with little human sympathy or kindness. So what was the use of observing all the rites and praying to the gods?" As Amita talks of her past, it is clear that she has been in a hostile clinch with her mother all her life. Amita went to see many gurus but was dissatisfied with every one of them till one day, a few years ago, she attended one of Mataji's public meetings. Her conversion was instantaneous, and she has remained a devoted disciple ever since. "Mataji is like the cloud that gives rain to everyone," she says. I am struck by the juxtaposition of her imagery in which mother is dry while Mataji brims over with the rain of love.

For Amita, then, Mataji's parental style has elements of both the familiar and the strange. The familiarity is in Mataji's fierceness, the "hot temper"; the difference, and this is indeed crucial, is in the preponderance of warmth and love in Mataji as compared to Amita's early experience of the indifference of her mother's "style." A guru like the late Maharaj Charan Singh of the Radhasoami sect, I would suggest, is too remote from Amita's central conflict, while the late Bhagwan Rajneesh, of Oregon and Pune fame, would be too threatening to the moral values of a girl brought up in an orthodox, middle-class Brahmin family. Mataji's parental style, on the other hand, dovetails with Amita's selfobject needs and social experience.

That the guru-disciple relationship is in important ways an extension of the parent-child relationship, constituting a developmental second chance for obtaining the required nutrients for the cohesion, integration, and vigorousness of the self, is implicit in some of the older devotional literature and is often explicitly stated by modern gurus. Basava, the twelfth-century founder of the Virsaiva sect, identifies the guru god with a particular aspect of the mother:

> As a mother runs
> Close behind the child
> With his hand on a cobra
> Or a fire
> The lord of meeting rivers
> Stays with me
> Every step of the way
> And looks after me.[23]

In his instructions to disciples, a contemporary guru, Swami Saty-anand Saraswati, tells us, "Now in relation with guru, the disciple chooses one *bhava* (emotional state) for himself, according to his personality and needs, and develops that to its fullest potential. If he feels the need for a friend, he should regard the guru as his friend. Or, if he has been lacking parental love, the guru can be his father and mother. . . . It all depends on your basic needs and which area of your personality is the most powerful. Sometimes in adopting a certain *bhava* toward the guru, the disciple tends to transfer his complexes and neurosis too. If he has become insecure due to the suffering meted out to him by harsh parents, then in relationship with guru too, he feels insecure."[24]

Swami Satyanand's remarks also tell us of the difficulties in the path of *surrender* to the guru, an emotional experience which is indispensable for mutative changes in the disciple's self.

If there is one demand made by the guru on the disciple, it is of surrender, an opening up and receptivity of the latter's psyche which is sometimes sought to be conveyed through (what men imagine to be) the imagery of female sexual experience. Saraswati writes, "When you surrender to the guru, you become like a valley, a vacuum, an abyss, a bottomless pit. You acquire depth, not height. This surrender can be felt in many ways. The guru begins to manifest in you; his energy begins to flow into you. The guru's energy is continuously flowing, but in order to receive it, you have to become a womb, a receptacle."[25]

Surrender of the self is, of course, ubiquitous in the religious traditions of the world. In his *The Varieties of Religious Experience*, William James called it regeneration by relaxing and letting go, psy-chologically indistinguishable from Lutheran justification by faith and the Wesleyan acceptance of free grace. He characterized it as giving one's private convulsive self a rest and finding that a greater self is there. "The results, slow or sudden, great or small, of the combined optimism and expectancy, the regenerative phenomenon which ensues on the abandonment of effort, remain firm facts of human nature." He added, . . . "you see why self-surrender has been and always must be regarded as the vital turning point of religious life. . . . One may say the whole development of Christianity in inwardness has consisted in little more than greater and greater emphasis attached to this crisis of self-surrender."[26]

In Sufism, too, surrender to the master is a necessary prerequisite for the state of *fana fil-shaykh* or annihilation of oneself in the master. Of the *iradah*, the relationship between the Sufi master and his disciple, the Sufi poet says: "O heart, if thou wanted the Beloved to be happy with thee, then thou must do and say what he commands. If he says, 'Weep blood!' do not ask 'Why?'; if He says, 'Die!' do not say 'How is that fitting?'"[27]

In terms of self psychology, surrender is the full flowering of the idealizing transference, with its strong need for the experience of merging into a good and powerful, wise and perfect selfobject—the guru. "This is the secret of the guru-disciple relationship," says one guru. "The Guru *is* the disciple, but perfected, complete. When he forms a relationship with the guru, the disciple is in fact forming a relationship with his own best self."[28] The disciple, in experiencing his or her self as part of the guru's self, hearing with the guru's ears, seeing with the guru's eyes, tasting with the guru's tongue, feeling with the guru's skin, may be said to be striving for some of the most archaic selfobject experiences.

Ramakrishna, the arch example of the Indian penchant for using narrative form in construction of a coherent and integrated world, of its preference for the language of the concrete, of image and symbol over more conceptual and abstract forms, tells us the following parable.

One day while driving with Arjuna (the warrior hero of the epic Mahabharata), Krishna (who is both God and Arjuna's guru) looked at the sky and said, "See, friend, how beautiful is the flock of pigeons flying there!" Arjuna saw it and immediately said, "Yes, friend, very beautiful pigeons indeed." The very next moment Krishna looked up again and said, "How strange, friend, they are by no means pigeons." Arjuna saw the birds and said,, "Quite so, my friend, they are not pigeons at all." "Now try to understand the matter," Ramakrishna exhorts us. "Arjuna's truthfulness is unquestionable. He could have never flattered Krishna in agreeing with him both the times. But Arjuna's devotional surrender to Krishna was so very great that he actually saw with his own eyes whatever Krishna saw with his."[29]

Devotees come to the guru, as do patients to the analyst, in a conflicted state. On the one hand, there is the unconscious hope of making up for missing or deficient selfobject responses in interaction with the guru. On the other hand, there is the fear of evoking self-fragmenting responses through the same interaction. The omnipresence of fears of injury to the self and of regression into early primitive states of self-dissolution is what forces the devotee to be wary of intimacy. It prevents the desired surrender to the guru however high the conscious idealization of the values of surrender and letting go might be. Gurus are of course aware of the conflict and in their various ways have sought to reassure the disciples about their fears. Muktananda, for instance, writes, "There are only two ways to live: One is with constant conflict, and the other is with surrender. Conflict leads to anguish and suffering. . . . But when someone surrenders with understanding and equanimity, his house, body and heart becomes full. His former feeling of emptiness and lack disappears."[30] And one of his disciples puts it in a language which the modern self psychologist would have no hesitation in acknowledging as his own: "We live in countless fleeting relationships, always seeking, finding and losing again. As children and adults, we learn through these relationships. We learn by taking into ourselves our loved ones' thoughts and voices, absorbing our loved ones' very presence along with their knowledge."[31] Gurus, gurus have always emphasized, are not human beings, not objects in the inelegant language of psychoanalysis, but functions. They are the power of grace in spiritual terms and intense selfobject experiences in the language of self psychology.

The psychological term "intense selfobject experience" of course transfers the location of the fount of "grace" from the person of the guru to the psyche of the devotee. It is a grace we have all experienced as infants when the mother's various ministrations transformed our internal world from states of disintegration to one of feeling integrated, from dreaded intimations of fragmentation to blissful experiences of wholeness. The persistent search for this inner metamorphosis in adult life is what makes the guru in India—to use Christopher Bollas' concept—a primary "transformational object."[32] He is the culturally sanctioned addressee of a collective request for the transforming experience which goes beyond healing in its narrow sense. The guru's grace is, then, the devotee's recollection of an earlier transformed state.

It is a remembrance, Bollas reminds us, which does not take place cognitively but existentially through intense affective experience, even when the latter is not on the same scale as in early life. The anticipation of being transformed by the guru inspires the reverential attitude toward his person, an attitude which in secular man, especially in the West, is more easily evoked by the transformational objects of art than those of religious faith.

The idealizing transference, leading to the merging experience, is thus the core of the healing process in the guru-disciple relationship. The healing is seen in terms of an alchemical transformation of the self: "When iron comes in contact with the philosopher's stone, it is transmuted in gold. Sandalwood trees infuse their fragrance into the trees around them."[33] Psychoanalysts, of the object relations and self psychology schools, will have no quarrel with this formulation of the basis of healing. Their model of the healthy person, however, requires an additional step—of reemergence; the drowning and the resurfacing are both constituents of psychological growth, at all developmental levels. In Kohut's language, healing will not only involve an ancient merger state but a further shift from this state to an experience of empathic resonance with the selfobject.

Gurus are generally aware of the dangers of self-fragmentation and the disciple's defenses against that dreaded inner state. Modern gurus, like Muktananda, talk explicitly about the agitation and anxiety a disciple may feel when he is close to the guru. The training required en route to surrender is hard and painful. Merger experience, they know, takes place not at once but in progressive stages as, for instance, depicted in Jnaneshvara's description of the unfolding of the guru-disciple relationship in the imagery of bridal mysticism.[34] They are aware of the resistances and the negative transferences, the times when the devotee loses faith in the guru, and doubts and suspicions tend to creep in. Do not break the relationship when this is happening, is the general and analytically sound advice. The development of inimical feelings toward the guru are part of the process of healing transformation. What is important about the feelings toward the guru is their strength, not their direction. Whether devoted or hostile, as long as the disciple remains turned toward the guru, he will be met by total acceptance. Muktananda describes the ideal guru's behavior: "A true guru breaks your old habits of fault finding, of seeing sin, of hating yourself. He roots out the negative seeds that you have sown as well as your feelings of guilt. . . . You will never hear the guru criticize you. Instead, when you are in his company, you will experience your own divinity. You will never be found guilty in the guru's eyes. You will find in them only the praise of your hidden inner God."[35]

The "ambience of affective acceptance" provided by the guru and his establishment, the *ashram*, will, the master knows, make the disciple feel increasingly safe, shifting the inner balance between need and fear toward the former. Old repressed and disavowed selfobject needs will reawaken and be mobilized, making the transference more and more intense. Or, put simply, as the conflict between need and fear recedes, the guru, like the analyst, will become the focus for the freshly released, though old, capacities for love, which push strongly toward a merger with the beloved.

If there is a second word besides surrender with which the guru-disciple relationship can be captured, it is *intimacy*. As Lawrence Babb remarks of his interviews with the devotees of Sai Baba, "What emerges as one general theme in these accounts is the same kind of visual, tactile and alimentary intimacy that is so central to devotional Hinduism in general. The devotees long to see him, to hear him, to be near him, to have private audiences with him, to touch him (especially his feet) and to receive or consume, or use in other ways, substances and objects that have been touched by him or that originate from him."[36] This striving for intimacy not only marks the disciple's response to the devotional, but also to the knowledge, guru. Pupul Jayakar, in talking of her response to the "intellectual" Krishnamurti, says "I was driven by the urge to be with him, to be noticed by him, to probe into the mysteries that pervaded his presence. I was afraid of what would happen, but I could not keep away."[37]

The sought-for intimacy is of an archaic nature, before the birth of language which separates and bifurcates. In the intimacy scale of the sixteenth-century North Indian saint Dadu:

> The guru speaks first with the mind
> Then with the glance of the eye
> If the disciple fails to understand
> He instructs him at last by word of mouth
> He that understands the spoken word is a common man
> He that interprets the gesture is an initiate
> He that reads the thought of the mind
> Unsearchable, unfathomable, is a god.[38]

In the desired preverbal intimacy with the guru, Jnaneshvara highlights the devotee's infantile quiescence.

To say nothing is your praise
To do nothing is your worship
To be nothing is to be near you.[39]

Analysts are, of course, familiar with the regressive movements in the patient's psyche occasioned by the growing transference toward the analyst. The regression gives the patient a double vision, both in relation to himself and to the analyst. Within the transference, he "sees" the analyst as a parental selfobject; in the real relationship as a helpful doctor. The two images, in flux over time, constantly condition each other. Because of the copresence of the patient's adult self, the illusion in relation to the analyst, though it waxes and wanes, remains more or less moderate.[40]

The patient's illusion of the analyst corresponds to another illusion in relation to the self. Patients in analysis often report feeling childlike, even childish, also outside the analytic setting. They imagine themselves at times to be smaller and more awkward than their actual adult selves. The infantile and the adult in relation to the self shape each other and are often in a state of partial identity. In the guru-disciple relationship, the identity between the actual and the infantile selves of the disciple on the one hand and the real and parental representations of the master on the other overlap to a much greater extent and for longer periods of time than in psychoanalysis. The double vision in relation to both self and guru representations tends to become monocular. In other words, the guru-disciple interaction touches deeper, more regressed layers of the psyche which are generally not reached by psychoanalysis. The devotee, I believe, is better (but also more dangerously) placed than the analysand to connect with—and correct—the depressive core at the base of human life from which a self first emerged and which lies beyond words and interpretations.

The healing techniques of the guru are thus designed to foster deeper regressions than those of the analyst. Elsewhere, I have talked of the importance of looking and being looked at as a primary technique of the master-disciple intercourse.[41] I discussed the identity-giving power of the eyes that recognize, that is, of their self-evoking and self-sustaining functions. Taken in through the eyes, the guru as a benign selfobject opens the devotee's closed world of archaic destructive relationships to new possibilities. The technical word, used in scriptural descriptions of the initiation process, is *darshanat*, "through the guru's look" in which, as Muktananda observes, "You are seen in every detail as in a clear mirror."[42] To the utter *clarity* of the look he might have added its absolute love and complete forgiveness. To adapt Dostoyevski's remark on the lover's vision, in *darshanat* the devotee is looked at, and is enabled to look at himself or herself, as God might have. Even gurus with thousands of disciples, whose devotees might conceivably doubt that a one-to-one recognition by the guru is taking place at regular intervals, are at pains to confirm the operation of *darshanat* in spite of the large numbers involved. To quote Muktananda again: "Many people become angry with me out of love. They say 'Baba did not look at me,' or 'When Baba looked at me, he didn't smile!' People who say these things do not understand that when I sit on my chair I look at everyone once, silently and with great joy. . . . True love has no language. If I look at someone, silently emitting a ray of love, that is sublime. This is true and should be understood: love is a secret ray of the eyes."[43]

What about the guru's words, the discourses to which the devotees listen with such rapt attention? To someone reading such a discourse or listening to it apart from a devotee group, it may seem trite, repetitious, and full of well-known homilies. The power of the guru's speech, however, lies not in its insight, but has a different source. "I did not understand but I came away with the words alive within me" is a typical reaction.[44] The psychological impact of the words is not through their literal meaning but their symbolic power, through the sound which conveys the experience of the guru's presence within the psyche. They are a form of early human contact, much as the experience of a child who is soothed by the mother's vocalizations even when he is physically separated from her and cannot feel her arms around him. In psychoanalysis, a patient will sometimes comment on the quality of the therapist's voice when he feels it as a psychological bridge which joins the two or when he feels it as distancing and evoking a self-fragmenting response. Susan Bady has suggested that it is not only the psychological reaction to the therapist's voice but its virtual ingestion by the patient in a concrete way which is significant.[45] Taken into one's vocal chords, the pattern and rate of breathing, the movement of the diaphragm, the relaxed and self-assured voice of the therapist or the guru will calm his agitation, infuse hope and courage into his own timid and hesitant voice.

The concrete physical and psychic manifestations of the guru's speech and sound are immeasurably enhanced by the group setting in which a disciple normally hears his words. To quote from my own experience of listening to a guru in a large crowd: "At first there is a sense of unease as the body, the container of our individuality and the demarcator of our spatial boundaries, is sharply wrenched from its habitual mode of experiencing others. For as we grow up, the touch of others, once so deliberately courted and responded to with delight, increasingly becomes ambivalent. Coming from a loved one, touch is deliciously welcomed; with strangers, on the other hand, there is an involuntary shrinking of the body, their touch taking on the menacing air of invasion by the other. But once the fear of touch disappears in the fierce press of other bodies and the individual lets himself become a part of the crowd's density, the original apprehension is gradually transformed into an expansiveness that stretches to include the others. Distances and differences—of status, age and sex—disappear in an exhilarating feeling (temporary to be sure) that individual boundaries can indeed be transcended and were perhaps illusory in the first place. Of course, touch is only one of the sensual stimuli that hammers at the gate of individual identity. Other excitations, channelled through vision, hearing and smell, are also very much involved. In addition, as Phyllis Greenacre has suggested, there are other, more subliminal exchanges of body heat, muscle tension and body rhythms taking place in a crowd. In short the crowd's assault on the sense of individual identity appears to be well-nigh irresistible; its invitation to a psychological regression—in which the image of one's body becomes fluid and increasingly blurred, controls over emotions and impulses are weakened, critical faculties and rational thought processes are abandoned—is extended in a way that is both forceful and seductive."[46]

Other techniques employed in the guru-disciple interaction perform a similar function of psychic loosening and fostering deep regression— an increasing surrender to the selfobject experience of the merging kind. The taking in of *prasada*, food offerings touched or tasted by the guru, drinking of the water used to wash his feet, helps in a loosening up of individual bodily and psychic boundaries, transforming the experience of the guru from that of a separate Other to one of comingling with a selfobject. Gurus and devotees have always known that meditation on the guru's face or form or the contemplative use of his photograph, as required in some cults, will contribute to and hasten the merging experience. As Muktananda observes: "The mind that always contemplates the guru eventually becomes the guru. Meditation on the guru's form, immerses the meditator in the state of the guru."[47]

In a sense, my use of the term guru-disciple interaction has been a misnomer since it has had the disciple's rather than the guru's inner state as its focus. Perhaps this is as it should be given the fact that ostensibly the disciple is the one in search of healing, and that we know infinitely more about the inner processes of disciples than those of the gurus. Yet an analyst has to wonder how a guru deals with the massive idealizing transferences of so many disciples. Negative transferences and malignant projections are of course easier to handle since they cause severe discomfort, compelling us to reject them by discriminating inside between what belongs to us and the alien attributes that have been projected onto us. This painful motivation for repelling the invasion of the self by others does not exist when projections are narcissistically gratifying, as they invariably are in case of the adoring followers.

The problem is further complicated by the fact that for the self-sustaining and self-healing responses to be evoked in the follower (or in the patient), the guru (and the analyst) must accept being the wiser, greater, and more powerful parent. To accept and yet not identify with the disciple's parental representation demands the guru remain in touch with his own infantile self. The best of the gurus, as we saw in the case of Ramakrishna, clearly do that; their own relationship to the Divine keeps intact self-representations other than those of the omniscient parent. But for many others, I would speculate, the temptation to identify with the disciple's projected parental self is overwhelming. As the parent and the stronger figure in the parent-child relationship, it is easier to unload one's conflicts and the depressive self onto the child. In the case of the analyst's countertransference, as Michael Moeller points out, the identification with the parental role is a source of twofold relief: one, in the transferential repetition of the relationship with the patient the analyst is the stronger and the less incriminated parent, and two, in reality he is not that parent at all.[48] The empirical finding on the antidepressive effect of the psychoanalytic role also applies to the guru. His calm, cheerful, loving mien is perhaps a consequence rather than a cause of his role as the healer.

I have mentioned above that the dangers of the guru role lie in the disciples' massive parental projections which the guru must process internally. Although the guru shares this danger with the analyst, or more generally, with any healer, the intensity of these projections, their duration, and the sheer number of devotees involved are vastly greater than in the case of his secular counterparts. These idealizing projections are subversive of the guru's self-representation, constitute an insidious assault which a few gurus—again like some therapists—are not able to successfully resist. A regression to an omnipotent grandiosity is one consequence, while in the sexual sphere a retreat into sexual perversion has been reported often enough to constitute a specific danger of the guru role. It is sad to hear or read reliable reports about seventy-year-old gurus who become Peeping-Toms as they arrange, with all the cunning of the voyeur, to spy on their teenaged female disciples (generally Western) undressing for the night in the *ashram*. The promiscuity of some other gurus, pathetically effortful in the case of elderly bodies with a tendency to flag, is also too well known to merit further repetition.

The sexual aberrations, however, have not only to do with pathological regression in stray individual cases, but are perhaps also facilitated by the way the fundamentals of healing are conceptualized in the guru-devotee encounter. For instance, given the significance of a specific kind of intimacy, there is no inherent reason (except cultural disapproval) why intimacy between guru and devotee does not progress to the most intimate encounter of all and be seen as a special mark of the guru's favor; why the merger of souls does not take place through their containers, the bodies. If substances which have been in intimate contact with the guru's body are powerful agents of inner change when ingested by the devotee, then the logic of transformation dictates that the most powerful transforming substance would be the guru's "purest" and innermost essence—his semen.

3

Psychoanalysis and Religion
Revisited

In conclusion, as I take up the wider issue of the relationship between psychoanalysis and religion, I do not propose to dwell overly long on Freud's well-known and essentially hostile view of religion. Freud believed that the common theme running through different aspects of religion—knowledge, belief, ritual, religious experience and feelings, ethical consequences in values and conduct—was an expression of the infantile in mental life. Religion was the way man defended himself against anxiety and the afflictions of an incomprehensible fate. Given Freud's stature and authority within the field, his views were to have a decisive influence on the way psychoanalysis, especially in its fledging years, approached religion. Occasionally Freud might have tried to relativize his position, as in his letter to Oskar Pfister on *The Future of an Illusion:* "Let us be quite clear on the point that the views expressed in my book form no part of analytic theory. They are my personal views, which coincide with those of many non-analysts and pre-analysts, but there are certainly many excellent analysts who do not share them. If I drew on analysis for certain arguments—in reality one argument—that need deter no one from using the non-partisan method of analysis for arguing the opposite view."[1] At another place Freud admitted that his study of religious belief was limited to that of the common man, and that he regretted having ignored "the rarer and more profound type of religious emotion as experienced by mystics and saints."[2] In this brief book, I have in a sense tried to address the outstanding psychoanalytic agenda on religion. By concentrating on the "more profound type of religious emotion" experienced by the mystic, I have attempted to complement Freud's analysis of the meaning of religion for the "common man" with the meaning it has for the saint.

Freud's rare disclaimers, perhaps attempts at protecting the sensitivities of his more spiritually inclined friends and admirers, did not prevent the emergence of a dominant psychoanalytic interpretation of religion. If there were disagreements among the early analysts with the master, they were on details rather than the essence of Freud's theoretical approach. Basic to this approach, of course, was the analogy between religious and psychopathological phenomena.

Religious *ideas*, for instance, the Judeo-Christian cosmogonies, were dubbed as illusory wish fulfillments. Their hold on man's imagination was seen as derived from the child's helplessness in face of a threatening external world on the one hand and his ambivalent feelings toward a father who is both a source of protection and fear on the other.[3]

Religious *rituals* were scathingly indicted through psychiatric diagnostic labels after Freud began the process by comparing the practices of the devout to the self-imposed restrictions of the obsessional neurotic.[4]

Religious *experience*, of which the mystical, "oceanic" feeling is widely held to be the standard bearer, we already saw in the first chapter, was a regression to the limitless primary narcissism of the infant united with the mother at the breast. Or, in more libidinal terms, Wilhelm Reich interpreted mystical experience as a misinterpretation of sexual feelings. The mystical response was a distorted sexuality which did not allow the perception of sexual excitation and precluded orgastic release.[5] (Let me add here that a Hindu tantrik in describing a vital part of his own practice would be in substantial agreement with Reich's formulation.) The inner world of religious *belief* too did not escape psychopathological analogy in being compared to amentia, a state of blissful, hallucinatory confusion.[6]

Well into the adult years of psychoanalysis as a discipline, many analysts would continue to follow Freud's lead. To give only one notorious instance: Franz Alexander, seeking a psychological understanding of the stages of meditation in Buddhism, discerned in them successive clinical pictures of melancholia, catatonic ecstasy, apathy, and schizophrenic dementia.[7] For him what motivates the Buddhist meditator is the attempt to regress to a condition of intrauterine existence. Even today, more than eighty years after Freud's first foray into religion in his 1907 article "Obsessive Actions and Religious Practices," the efforts by psychoanalysts to move the religious world with the lever of psychopathology have not been given up. In Jeffrey Masson's 1980 study of Indian religious traditions, for example, much of Buddhism was seen as a massive defense against depression while the Hindu tantrik's desire for stillness, echoing Wilhelm Reich, was traced to early fears of sexual excitement.[8]

There are numerous other instances within the psychoanalytic literature where the significance of the analogy between religious and psychopathological phenomena is not questioned. The writers share Freud's original assumption that the meaning of the likeness between the two is unambiguous. But as the French philosopher Paul Ricouer remarks, "Analysis does indeed throw some light on what we have called the birth of idols; but it has no way of deciding whether that is all that faith is; whether ritual is originally, in its primordial function, obsessional ritual; whether faith is merely consolation on the childhood pattern. Analysis can reveal to the religious man his caricature, but it leaves him the task of meditating on the *possibility* of not resembling his distorted double."[9] From within the ranks of the analysts, Erik Erikson voices a similar concern when in speaking of religious striving he rhetorically asks, "But must we call it regression if man thus seeks again the earliest encounters of his trustful past in his efforts to reach a hoped for and eternal future?"[10]

Even in the early years, besides apostates like Jung, there were the so-called revisionist, neo-Freudians like Erich Fromm and Karen Horney who tried to bridge the gulf between analysis and religion. To them the convergence between the two, the common agenda of both psychoanalysis and religion, lay in the healing of man's soul. After all, as Bruno Bettelheim has demonstrated, Freud's writings in their original German, though excised in English translation, are full of references and matters pertaining to the soul—its nature and structure, its development and attributes, and the way the soul reveals itself in all we do and dream.[11] Freud's own text is full of rich ambiguities, his terminology often open-ended and allusive, his tone personal and conversational. In the translation such qualities are played down for the sake of an abstract, medicalized "scientific language" using ancient Greek and Latin words. As a *Seelenartzt*, not a doctor of the mind or of the *Nerven*, what the analyst clearly does is minister to the soul. Of course, the Freudian analyst, first and foremost a psychologist of love, conceives of the soul in a particular, erotic way that is akin to the mythic psyche of the Greeks, a butterfly eternally pursued by an indefatigable Cupid.

For Fromm, who was part of a stubborn nonmedical tradition within psychoanalysis which persists to this day, though perhaps less in the United States than in other countries, what a successful and effective analysis achieved above all was to awaken the patient's sense of wondering and questioning. Ideally, it brought to life a capacity for being genuinely bewildered, called forth an engagement with what the theologian Paul Tillich called "ultimate concern." The neurotic, in the view of both Horney and Fromm passionately concerned with the fulfillment of his own desires, always aimed at the absolute, the unlimited, and the infinite. In this he was the antithesis of the truly religious man for whom only for God everything is possible. As Horney put it, "The neurotic is the Faust who is not satisfied with knowing a great deal, but has to know everything."[12] He is at the opposite pole from the well-functioning man—religious and psychoanalytic—who has a vision of possibilities while at the same time he realizes the limitation of necessities, and of the concrete.

The convergence of the psychoanalytic and the religious man requires, of course, a particular vision of religion (and of psychoanalysis) which Fromm called "humanist religion".[13] He professed to see it pervading early Buddhism, Taoism, and Jewish and Christian mysticism. In contrast to what he termed "authoritarian" religion, the aim of humanist religion is fullest self-realization and the achievement of greatest inner strength. Authoritarian religion, on the other hand, wanted man to submit and surrender to a transcendent power. It extolled obedience, reverence, and worship of a higher entity. In advancing the ideals of knowledge, brotherly love, reduction of suffering, independence, and responsibility, Freud articulates the ethical core of humanist religion. Jung, on the other hand, according to Fromm, though apparently a greater friend of religion, emphasized man's helplessness and seizure by powers higher than himself and is thus at best a spokesman for authoritarian religion.

The distinction between two kinds of religion, the one a mature faith with which psychoanalysis has no quarrel and whose aims it even shares, and the second a system of infantile belief and neurotic ritual, continued to be made in essentially similar terms by a few writers on the psychology of religion. Abraham Kaplan's contrasting of infantile religion with a mature version which emphasizes responsibility rather than dependency, anxiety, and guilt, Harry Guntrip's description of mature religiosity based on the experience of meaningful human relationships, and Peter Homans' opposition between "transference God" and a nonpathological religion of transcendence, all are some examples.[14] In the same vein, Ricouer has contrasted infantile and idolatrous consolation with a consolation "according to spirit" which, evoking shades of Horney, is free of all narcissism and self-seeking.[15] Though in no way providing a refuge from the harshness of existence, the consolation according to spirit is acquired in extreme obedience to reality—the psychoanalytic God—and can only emerge from the ashes of the first consolation.

Starting from the late 1950s, there have been voices within the mainstream of Freudian psychoanalysis which too have attempted to articulate a new approach to religion. Instead of harping on the resemblance between unconscious id impulses and elements of religious myths and ritual, these analysts sought to elaborate on the ways religion strengthens and support the ego and thus serves adaptive rather than defensive purposes in human maturation. Sympathetic to or associated with the American school of ego psychology, which emphasizes adaptation and not only conflict, their approach was closer to that of anthropology where in spite of a few reports that describe anxiety-generating aspects of ritual or the dysphoric impact of religious participation, the leitmotif within the field has been the psychologically integrative function of religion. The ego psychologists interested in religious phenomena, Jacob Arlow and Erik Erikson being perhaps the foremost, recognized that religious knowledge incorporated in myths provided the ego opportunities for mastery through a healing identification with the central figures of the myth.[16] Rituals were viewed as communal experience of special import, "ceremonial dreams of great recuperative value" as Erikson called them,[17] which support the ego in its struggle against id impulses.

The influence of the ego psychologists, however, has remained confined to the United States, and here too it has made itself felt more in scholarly disciplines outside psychoanalysis. Freud's legacy, which holds that gods, both in the inner world of the individual and in the cultural universe of communities, have clay feet and that psychoanalysis, if it is to remain psychoanalysis, must of necessity be iconoclastic in its encounter with religion, has remained much too strong to be modified in any significant way.

Even while acknowledging iconoclasm as the specific contribution of psychoanalysis to the study of cultural phenomena, one is puzzled by the inconsistencies in its application. For instance, again following Freud, the respect accorded to art and the combination of benevolence and admiration with which the artist is regarded in psychoanalytic writings, even while his deeper motivations are being scrutinized, is strikingly absent from studies of religion and the *homo religiosi*. Creativity is granted to the writer and the painter while all psychoanalytic virtue is denied to the mystic.

The harshness of the psychoanalytic discourse toward religion, especially in the early years of its establishment as a clinical method and intellectual discipline, has two roots. The first goes back to the person of the founder of psychoanalysis and the second to the intellectual compulsions and ideologies of the historical era in which psychoanalysis was born and struggled to establish itself as a profession. Freud has taught us that an individual's passionately held ideas and convictions are not autonomous from his unconscious needs and conflicts, and analysts have not hesitated to apply this lesson to Freud's own views and complex relationship with religion. Gregory Zilboorg, for instance, comes to the conclusion that Freud struggled with unresolved religious conflict and that his vehement denouncements revealed repressed, deeply religious convictions.[18] Others too have discerned in Freud a deep ambivalence toward religion which might lead some to conclude that Freud was more a closet than a godless Jew.

Freud himself was too much of an analyst to ignore the possibility of the existence of a relationship between his conception of religion and his deeper motivations, though he chose to pass over the possible connections without conducting a searching public examination. Thus in a letter to Pfister he writes, "Of course it is very possible that I might be mistaken on all three points, the independence of my theories from my disposition, the validity of my arguments on their behalf, and their content. You know that the more magnificent the prospect the lesser the certainty and the greater the passion—in which we do not wish to be involved—with which men take sides."[19]

The focal unconscious conflict which some students of Freud believe to have identified is his ambivalence toward the mother of the earliest years of his life and the persistence of preoedipal influences and residues in his inner world.[20] These are also reflected in the directions taken by his work. Till well into the mid-1930s, Freud's writings did not take the infant's early experience of its mother fully into account, though toward the end his recognition of the impact of the mother on mental life was coming closer to conscious toleration. The ambivalence toward the maternal feminine began to ease as he was inexorably pulled into the embrace of the *ewigweibliche*, the eternal feminine. Irving Harrison relates Freud's pivotal conflict to the first three years of his life when he lived with his parents in a one-room house.[21] Here, in cramped quarters, following Sigmund's birth, two siblings were conceived and born, and one died. The exposure to the intense stimulation of the first three years, not only in the repeated excitement at being a witness to the primal scene but also through the contagious effect of strong effects experienced by the parents, including the grief at the death of a child, molded Freud's particular area of psychic vulnerability.

On the one hand, this psychic space is filled with the diffuse, yet abiding and beckoning, presence of the adoring mother who bequeaths to her favorite son what Nabokov in his memoirs called "unreal estate," the special pleasures of childhood, the minutiae of utterly precise sensations, especially piquant and intense because they are as yet uncategorized, without the conceptual order that levels novelty into predictability. "A child's emotional impulses," Freud was to write, "are intensely and inexhaustibly deep to a degree quite other than those of an adult; only religious ecstasy can bring them back."[22] Yet perhaps for Freud the emotions associated with the preoedipal mother to be brought back to awareness also meant the rising to the surface of the "horror of abandonment, the awareness of siblings as occupying his mother and contributing to that abandonment and the raging wish that all sources of such terror cease to be."[23]

In some of his writings on religion, for example, in *Moses and Monotheism*, it has been suggested that Freud's focal conflict is reflected in his stubbornly held notion of an archaic heritage of primeval parricide which obscures and bypasses the maternal aspects of monotheistic religions.[24] And if religious feeling begins with the wonder, magic, and maternal awe of the child's early years, to ripen into the mature faith of adulthood that can engage with "ultimate concern," then Freud's private religion remained at an archaic level. A fascination with the occult, with mysterious psychical phenomena and a tendency toward what is called superstition, accompanied him through a major part of his life. In his biography, Ernst Jones noted that Freud once wrote but then forgot and later denied: "If I had my life to live over again I should devote myself to psychical research rather than psychoanalysis."[25] We also know that despite his dismissal of mysticism, Freud was strongly attracted toward men with a mystical bent—Jung, Rolland, and even Flies with his numerological theories—extending to them a reverence he normally reserved for creative artists. Harrison links Freud's personal conflict, his treatment of religion, and the birth of psychoanalysis even more intimately when he observes, "How tempting to any man harboring such latent potential for terrors and rages must be the mystical vision of regaining total bliss—of the ocean as a womb! And psychoanalysis, for all its selective inattention to that theme, may have been born of Freud's resolute determination to resist just that temptation."[26]

I have attributed the second reason for the analytic antagonism toward religion to the historical origins of psychoanalysis. Its pioneers were steeped in a European culture where the sense of the sacred was fast disappearing and *disenchantment*, as Max Weber called the loss, had spread far and wide in the wake of capitalism and the industrial revolution. In fact, Peter Homans has directly linked the very origins of psychoanalysis to the creative response of Freud and other early analysts to this loss, to their ability to mourn the withering away of traditional forms of community life and long-cherished values, including, after the carnage of the First World War, the values of German liberalism.[27]

In any event, the birth of psychoanalysis took place "under a planetary constellation" (an astrologically inclined Hindu would say) when rationalism was the preeminent current of the intellectual climate and the ideology of positivism reigned unchallenged in the sciences. Though religion and psychoanalysis may have looked at a similar universe, the former, according to Freud, was a mythological view of the world while the psychoanalytic Weltanschauung was modern and scientific. Freud was hopeful of replacing religious knowledge by the psychological science he was in the process of forging. "In point of fact I believe that a large part of the mythological view of the world which extends a long way into most modern religions is nothing but psychology projected into the external world. The obscure recognition [the endopsychic perception] of psychical factors and relations in the unconscious is mirrored in the construction of a supernatural reality, which is destined to be changed back once more by science into the psychology of the unconscious. One could venture to explain in this way the myths of paradise and the fall of man, of God, of good and evil, of immortality, and so on, and to transform metaphysics into metapsychology."[28]

The respectability and recognition as a positivistic science which psychoanalysis claimed for itself was not to be won so easily in spite of the analogies and metaphors from the physical sciences that peppered Freud's writings. Its practice, the healing of *Seelenstörungen*— disturbances of the soul—was too near that of the numerous occultists and faith healers who operated at the fringes of the established churches. For intellectuals, scholars, and men of science, psychoanalysis was not so far removed from the animal magnetism of another Viennese healer with an international reputation, Franz Anton Mesmer, or from the endeavors of various spiritualists—phrenologists, Christian Scientists, and others—who sought to cloak religious concerns in scientific trappings. As late as 1932, Stefan Zweig, a great admirer of Freud, apologetically wrote in the introduction to his book *On Mental Healers* (*Die Heilung durch Den Geist*) that he hopes he won't be "accused of being a Mesmerist or a Christian Scientist or a devotee of psychoanalysis."[29]

There were other, more concrete manifestations in the practice of psychoanalysis which appeared to be directly derived from religious practices. For instance, the setting of psychoanalysis, with the analyst sitting outside the visual field of the patient, was uncomfortably similar to that of the priest hearing confession. The importance of the doctor establishing a good rapport with the patient had been earlier stressed by St. Ignatius of Loyola, the founder of the order of the Jesuits, as vital for the work of an effective spiritual director.

A traditional Hindu or Buddhist, on the other hand, would point out even more parallels. In the practice of psychoanalysis he would see a modern form of the master-disciple relationship which has the personal transformation of the disciple as its goal. In its method of free association he would discern a rational meditation, with goals different from its religious counterpart and striking only insofar as the meditation is more joint than solitary. He may even go so far as to characterize psychoanalysis as "a secular Western counterpart to Tantra." He may also acknowledge that psychoanalysis has developed a specific and a most elaborate theory of *karma*—the influence of the past on the present—which has no rival in his own traditional canons either in subtlety or in sophistication.

Coming back to the Judeo-Christian tradition, the method of psychoanalysis, an introspective free association, was too close to older techniques of introspection and self-interrogation which drew their sustenance from religion and which were in the process of withering away. Many scientists and other educated men would have agreed with George Steiner's comment that "It [psychoanalysis] provides a secular, though heavily mythological surrogate for an entire range of introspective and elucidatory disciplines extending from private meditation to the metaprivacies of the confessional."[30] It then becomes understandable that psychoanalysis would seek to sharply demarcate its boundaries and differentiate its methods from comparable religious techniques which antedate it so vastly in the history of human consciousness. It also becomes understandable that there may have been lingering fears of psychoanalysis being taken over by religion. Of his book *The Future of an Illusion,* Freud would write that in this work he wished to protect psychoanalysis from the priests and entrust it "to a profession that doesn't yet exist, a profession of secular ministers of soul who don't have to be physicians and must not be priests."[31]

Today, in the last decade of the twentieth century, the compulsions I have described and which shaped the relationship of psychoanalysis to religion have largely disappeared. First, there is no longer the same concern with establishing psychoanalysis as a science in the positivist sense. There is an acceptance among analysts, of all persuasions, that psychoanalytic theory cannot be proven by experimental means and that research methods which take psychoanalysis out of its natural context cannot but distort its essence. There is a growing consensus that accurate predictions about a multidetermined human behavior cannot be made. Like the quantum universe of physics and unlike its Newtonian predecessor, the universe of psychoanalysis is of the interconnection between the subjectivities of the analyst and the analysand, and it is precisely the analyst's participation which makes it impossible to speak of either the absolute subjectivity or the absolute objectivity of the discipline. Whereas Freud, forced by the prevailing view of science which made a sharp demarcation between subject and object, felt compelled to distinguish between fantasy and reality, between *Dichtung* and *Wahrheit*, we no longer need to make this distinction quite so sharply and in fact, as we shall see, must not even formulate the question in the same way.

If today psychoanalysis aspires to be scientific at all it is only through keeping alive a questioning, searching attitude that would ideally breakfast every morning on a discredited theory. It is scientific in its continuous struggle, not always successful, to avoid falling prey to dogmas, irrespective of the authority or charisma of their propounders. No longer afraid to be called a hermeneutic enterprise, a *Geisteswissenschaft* of meaning rather than a natural science of causation, that is, a soul physics, psychoanalysis can contentedly exist in the boundary space between science and art and religion without feeling the need to accede to any one of them. Today, as Bion has observed, "it is as absurd to criticize a piece of psychoanalytic work on the ground that it is 'not scientific' as it is to criticize it because it is 'not religious' or 'not artistic'."[32]

The bypassing of the preoedipal mother which perhaps gave Freud's writings on religion their particular slant has since been amply rectified. In the work of many post- Freudians—such as Klein, Winnicott, Mahler, Kohut, Erikson—the Great Mother looms so large as not only to complement Freud's awesome father but to almost set up a parallel regime. In the "relational" models of the post-Freudians, it is not the derivatives of instinctual drives but the mental representations of relationships with others which constitute the fundamental building blocks of mental life.[33] Fragments of experiences with parents and other adults, images and fantasies of one's self in relation with others, and inner voices derived from these real and imagined experiences become the stuff of the self.

The pivotal relationship in the many relational theories, the basic building block of the self, is the infant-mother dyad at the beginning of life. Religion then gets connected to the origins of sentient life and the preoedipal experience. Winnicott, for instance, links religion to what he calls transitional phenomena in mental life.[34] These begin with the infant's transition from a state of being merged with the mother to a state of being in relation to the mother as something outside and separate. They are located in an intermediate space between inside and outside, between the subjective and what is objectively perceived, between the baby's inability and growing ability to recognize and accept reality. Winnicott sees transitional space as a resting place for the individual engaged in the perpetual human task of keeping inner and outer reality separate yet interrelated.

Relational theorists who seek to describe the ineffability of our earliest experience before language is born are often poetical—even Melanie Klein with her violent surrealistic images of breasts that persecute or/are filled with urine and feces. Winnicott calls transitional phenomena "the substance of illusion," the realm which is allowed to the infant and in adult life is inherent in art and religion. "The intermediate area of experience," Winnicott writes, "unchallenged in respect of its belonging to inner or external (shared) reality, constitutes the greater part of the infant's experience and throughout life is retained in the intense experiencing that belongs to the arts, and to religion and to imaginative living, and to creative scientific work."[35] By "unchallenged" Winnicott means that an essential part of the formulation of transitional phenomena is "that we agree never to make the challenge to the baby: did you create this object, or did you find it conveniently lying around? That is to say, an essential feature of transitional phenomena and objects is a *quality in our attitude* when we observe them."[36]

The presence of this particular "quality in attitude" in observation of religious phenomena distinguishes most relational theorists from their more classical predecessors and contemporaries. Erikson is not being reductionist when he links one face of religion to a dim nostalgia for a hallucinatory sense of unity with the maternal matrix and for a supply of benevolently powerful substances.[37] Noting man's wish for transcendence he does not proceed to reduce transcendence, but elevates the status of the wish. Nor does Kohut subscribe to a deterministic scientism when he would have religion as a cultural selfobject which provides vital nutrients for the maturation and maintenance of the self.[38]

Similarly, relational theories would interpret other areas of religion, such as methods of religious healing, quite differently from the classical drive model. For instance, taking an example from Hinduism, let us look at the silent "looking" of *darshan*, which I have described in the previous chapter as the most important form of interaction between the guru and the disciple, the chief healing technique if you will.[39] The classical analytic understanding of the self and an insight into its workings in the analytic situation is through verbalization. Words are the carriers of the knowledge that heals. Silence and quiescence are most often interpreted as resistance, defensive inhibition, or an ego disturbance of shorter or longer duration.

In the relational models, where the avoidance of a sense of estrangement and abandonment is deemed to be one of the primary motivational thrusts in the individual, the identity-giving powers of the eyes that *recognize* are at least as crucial as words that explain and integrate diffuse experience. In the silent affirmation of every *darshan*, the individual experiences in the guru the caretaker of his "prehistoric" era and a brief but regular fulfillment of a profound human need for mutual recognition. Taken in through the eyes, the guru is gradually internalized as a benign figure who is different from the disciple's bad inner objects and who opens the disciple's closed world of archaic and destructive object relationships to new possibilities.

That the silence of *darshan* works better in India than in the West may have to do with the caretaking patterns of the culture. In most Western societies, a large part of reassurance against the separation anxiety of childhood is provided by the mother's voice, for instance, at bedtime. Sleep itself means darkness, silence and—in most middle-class sleeping arrangements—separation from the mother so that silence becomes associated with the fear of her absence. In India, on the other hand, the child is almost constantly carried on the mother's body and sleeps at night with the mother in the same bed. Silence and quiescence may well be associated with the mother's presence and a union with the deep rhythms of her body. The analyst of relational models will thus admit to a certain affinity with the guru in that they share recognizable features of a common ancestry based on what evolution has created: human development embedded in a web of human connectedness, the self as a locus of relationships.

With greater awareness of the meaning and function of its own rituals, psychoanalysis can now appreciate religious ritual in a way more differentiated than was possible in Freud's early formulations. Every analyst is keenly cognizant of the importance of keeping the analytic atmosphere and setting constant. He or she is aware of the feeling of fragmentation in the patient, even if mild and fleeting, when the rituals of greeting and leave-taking are varied or the regularity of the sessions disturbed. Analytic ritual, when good, repeatedly confirms the personal bond between the patient and the analyst. It thus allows the patient to approach conflict and contradiction within an environment whose familiar interdependency has been stressed again and again. Like Thomas Mann's sartorial advice to the imaginative writer to dress like a bank clerk, the outer formalization of the analytic session fosters inner spontaneity. Of course, when the ritual, analytic or religious, is "bad", that is, when its repetiveness has become forced, rigid, and bereft of all spontaneity, it is then that Freud's analysis of ritual regains a certain validity.

Besides suggestive parallels and interesting convergences between religious ritual, spiritual techniques of self-interrogation, and psychoanalysis, what can push psychoanalysis away from its current habitat in the boundary space between science, art, and religion and toward declaring its alliance with religion is its mythic core. By this I do not mean that myths, such as that of Oedipus, which for most people now is more a Freudian than a Greek myth, build the core of psychoanalytic theory. Nor do I wish to highlight the concerns with origins, transformations, shifting realities—basically with meaning—that psychoanalysis shares with mythology. By mythic, of course, I do not mean fictional, the common meaning of myth in every European language since Plato pronounced it to be so. Mythic refers more to a certain structure of thought and reflection which serves to organize inner and outer experience. This particular structure, both at the heart of mythology and psychoanalysis, has fantasy as its foundation. Fantasy is again not used in the ordinary sense of the word with its popular connotations of whimsy, eccentricity, or triviality, but as another name for that world of imagination which seeks to give meaning to experience. Fantasy, "the stuff that dreams are made of," is to different extents and in different forms also the stuff out of which works of art, scholarly discourses, and scientific theories are constructed.

The intricate encasement of fantasy by symbolism, metaphor and analogy—the mythic structure of thought—is the source of the power of psychoanalytic theories as also its practice where it pervades the interweaving of the patient's productions with the analyst's responses, his interpretations. Ava Siegler has suggested that Freud's extensive use of metaphor and analogy in the development and expression of his ideas is not incidental but necessary to the explanatory power of his theories.[40] "Metaphor and analogy enable possibilities for complex orderings of knowledge. They can be used to help explain perception that would be difficult to explain otherwise. . . . Additionally, metaphor and analogy share an attribute of ambiguity. It is in their very nature to participate in and transfer excess or surplus meaning from one perception to another, enriching our understanding of subtle and intricate human experiences."[41]

Metaphor and analogy are not only integral to psychoanalytic theory but also to its practice. Even the conveying of analytic insight through interpretation, I believe, must not be crystal clear but to some extent overlapping and overinclusive. Like myths, the truly transmuting analytic insights exceed the language used to convey them, setting up resonances that reveal ever more hidden depths. Contrary to Freud's expectations, it is not the scientific worldview with its language of denotation, but the mythological Weltanschauung with connotation marking *its* language, which is a better path into the depths of emotion and imagination—the subject of psychoanalysis. Corresponding more to that which Oliver Sacks suggests is the iconical and "artistic" organization of the final form of the brain's record of experience and action, the mythic is truer to the melodic and scenic nature of inner life, to the Proustian nature of memory and mind.[42]

In summary, then, my own stance acknowledges the many significant similarities between psychoanalysis and religious healing and ordains the adoption of a different "quality in attitude" in the observation of religious phenomena. It certainly does not go as far as Wilfred Bion, a cult figure for many analysts, especially in Latin America, for whom the goals of psychoanalysis are mystical goals, and who deliberately takes recourse to religious terminology to describe what happens in a psychoanalysis. Bion would not rest content with the analysand's *knowing* of the phenomena of his real self but would ideally have him or her pass from knowing to *being* the real self.[43] This gap, Bion would say, can only be bridged by the "godhead" of the analysand consenting to be incarnated in his or her person. He would ideally suspend memory and desire to promote the exercise of the aspects of psyche that have no background in sensuous experience.

Though attracted and intrigued, I would prefer to remain with sensuous experience and the body, the only container we have of our souls. I would agree that the goal of analysis is setting free and greatly increasing the capacity for "experiencing experience" but would not ignore the sensual nature of experience, of having consciousness suffuse every part of one's body. To adapt one of Bion's own metaphors, I would be content to grow, dig out, and eat potatoes, intensely and sensuously, while admiring from afar, without doubting it, the mystic's ability to sing potatoes.

Notes

Chapter 1

1. N. Söderblom, *Till mystikens belysning* (Lund, 1985), cited in H. Akerberg, "The Unio Mystica of Teresa of Avila," in N.G. Holm, ed., *Religious Ecstasy* (Stockholm: Almqvist and Wiksell, 1981), 275–79.

2. William James, *The Varieties of Religious Experience* (New York: Longmans, Green, 1902).

3. Andrew M. Greeley, *The Sociology of the Paranormal: A Reconnaissance* (Beverly Hills: Sage Publications, 1975), 62.

4. For a psychological description of the structure of mystical experience see Committee on Psychiatry and Religion, *Mysticism: Spiritual Quest or Psychic Disorder?* (New York: Group for Advancement of Psychiatry, 1976). See also H. Hof, "Ecstasy and Mysticism," in Holm, *Religious Ecstasy*, 243–49.

5. R.C. Zaehner, *Hindu and Muslim Mysticism* (London: Athalone Press, 1960). The authoritative work on Hindu mysticism remains S.N. Dasgupta (1927), *Hindu Mysticism* (Delhi: Motilal Banarsidas, 1987).

6. See Committee on Psychiatry and Religion, *Mysticism*, especially 782–86. For specific psychoanalytic contributions stressing the ego-adaptive aspects of the mystic experience see Paul C. Horton, "The Mystical Experience: Substance of an Illusion," *Journal of the American Psychoanalytic Association* 22 (1974): 364–80; David Aberbach, "Grief and Mysticism," *International Review of Psychoanalysis* 14 (1987): 509–26.

7. Anton Ehrenzweig, *The Hidden Order of Art* (London: Weidenfeld and Nicolson, 1967).

8. Romain Rolland, *The Life of Ramakrishna* (Calcutta: Advaita Ashram, 1986), 38.

9. For the arguments against a psychoanalytic, "scientific" study of mysticism, see Roger N. Walsh et al., "Paradigms in Collision," in *Beyond Ego: Transpersonal Dimensions in Psychology*, ed. R.N. Walsh and F. Vaughan (Los Angeles: Tarcher, 1980), 36–52.

10. See Peter Buckley and Marc Galanter, "Mystical Experience, Spiritual Knowledge, and a Contemporary Ecstatic Experience," *British Journal of Medical Psychology* 52 (1979): 281–89.

11. For the case histories see P.C. Horton, "Mystical Experience," and Committee on Psychiatry and Religion, *Mysticism*, 799–807.

12. For a comprehensive comparison of the three see Manfred Eigen, "The Area of Faith in Winnicott, Lacan and Bion," *International Journal of Psychoanalysis* 62 (1981): 413–34.

13. Cited in Irving B. Harrison, "On Freud's View of the Infant-Mother Relationship and of the Oceanic Feeling—Some Subjective Influences," *Journal of the American Psychoanalytic Association* 27 (1979): 409.

14. Ibid.

15. J.M. Masson suggests a different passage from the writings of Ramakrishna as the source for the term "oceanic feeling"; see his *The Oceanic Feeling: The Origins of Religious Sentiment in Ancient India* (Dordrecht: Reidel, 1980), 36.

16. Dushan Pajin, "The Oceanic Feeling: A Reevaluation" (Belgrade, 1989, manuscript).

17. Letter to R. Rolland, 19 January 1930, in E. Freud, ed., *The Letters of Sigmund Freud* (New York: Basic Books, 1960), 392.

18. Mahendranath Gupta, *Sri Ramakrishna Vachanamrita*, trans. into Hindi by Suryakant Tripathi "Nirala," 3 vols. (Nagpur: Ramakrishna Math, 1988).

19. Swami Saradananda, *Sri Ramakrishna, The Great Master*, 2 vols. (Mylapore: Sri Ramakrishna Math, 1983), vol. 1, 276–77.

20. Rolland, *Life of Ramakrishna,* 22–23.

21. Saradananda, *Sri Ramakrishna,* vol. 1, 276–77

22. Ibid., 156

23. Ibid., 162–63.

24. Saradananda, *Sri Ramakrishna,* vol. 1, 424

25. Gupta, *Vachanamrita*, vol. 1, 71.

26. Ibid., 301.

27. Ibid., 320.

28. Ibid., 135–36.

29. Ibid., 41.

30. Ibid., vol. 2, 241.

31. Bhavabhuti, *Uttara Rama Charita*, in *Six Sanskrit Plays* (Bombay: Asia, 1964), 368.

32. Gupta, *Vachanamrita*, vol. 1, 90.

33. S. Freud, *New Introductory Lectures* (1933), *Standard Edition*, vol. 22, 79–80.

34. Nathaniel Ross, "Affect as Cognition: With Observation on the Meaning of Mystical States," *International Review of Psychoanalysis* 2 (1975): 79–93.

35. Gupta, *Vachanamrita*, vol. 3, 238–89.

36. Ernst Hartmann, *The Nightmare: The Psychology and Biology of Terrifying Dreams* (New York: Basic, 1984).

37. Gupta *Vachanamrita*, vol. 3, 289.

38. J.M.R. Damas Mora et al., "On Heutroscopy or the Phenomenon of the Double," *British Journal of Medical Psychology* 53 (1980): 75–83.

39. Gupta, *Vachanamrita*, vol. 1, 388.

40. Ibid., vol. 3, 109.

41. Ibid., vol. 1, 431.

42. Saradananda, *Sri Ramakrishna*, vol. 1, 417.

43. Octavio Paz, *The Money Grammarian*, trans. Helen Lane (New York: Seaver Books, 1981), 133.

44. For representative statements of the classical Freudian view see L. Salzman, "The Psychology of Religious and Ideological Conversion, " *Psychiatry* 16 (1953): 177–87. For the Kleinian view see Irving B. Harrison, "On the Maternal Origins of Awe," *The Psychoanalytic Study of the Child* 30 (1975): 181–95.

45. P.C. Horton, "Mystical Experience".

46. For a detailed discussion of the link and parallels between the process of mourning and mysticism see Aberbach, "Grief and Mysticism," 509–26.

47. S. Kakar, *Shamans, Mystics and Doctors* (New York: Knopf, 1982), chap. 5. See also Buckley and Galanter, "Mystical Experience," 285; P.C. Horton, "The Mystical Experience as a Suicide Preventive," *American Journal of Psychiatry* 130 (1973): 294–96.

48. Cited in Aberbach, "Grief and Mysticism," 509.

49. I. Barande and R. Barande, "Antinomies du concept de perversion et epigenese de l'appetit de excitation", cited in S.A. Leavy, "Male Homosexuality Reconsidered," *International Journal of Psychoanalytic Psychotherapy* 11 (1985–86), 163.

50. Gupta, *Vachanamrita*, vol. 1, 388.

51. Eigen, "Area of Faith"; "Ideal Images, Creativity and the Freudian Drama," *Psychocultural Review* 3 (1979): 278–98; "Creativity, Instinctual Fantasy and Ideal Images," *Psychoanalytic Review* 68 (1981).

52. Eigen, "Area of Faith," 431.

53. E. Underhill, *Mysticism* (1911) (New York: E.P. Dutton, 1961); J.H. Leuba, *The Psychology of Religious Mysticism* (New York: Harcourt, Brace, 1925).

54. A. Einstein, *Ideas and Opinions* (New York: Crown Publishers, 1954), 75.

55. Herbert Moller, "Affective Mysticism in Western Civilization," *Psychoanalytic Review* 52 (1965): 259–67. See also E.W. McDonnel, *The Beguines and Beghards in Medieval Culture* (New Brunswick: Rutgers University Press, 1954), 320–32.

56. Gupta, *Vachanamrita*, 3: 535–36.

57. Ibid., 107.

58. Robert Stoller, "The Gender Disorders," in I. Rosen, ed., *Sexual Deviation* (Oxford: Oxford University Press, 1979), 109–38.

59. J.O. Wisdom, "Male and Female," *International Journal of Psychoanalysis* 64 (1983): 159–68.
60. D.W. Winnicott, "Creativity and Its Origins," in *Playing and Reality* (London: Tavistock, 1971), 72–85.
61. Ibid., 85.

Chapter 2

1. Pupul Jayakar, *J. Krishnamurti: A Biography* (Delhi: Penguin, 1987), 9. Here I must add the caution contained in Brent's observation that "In a country where there are perhaps ten million holy men, many with their own devotees, acolytes and disciples, some of them gurus with hundreds of thousands of followers, all of them inheritors of a tradition thousands of years old, nothing that one can say about them in general will not somewhere be contradicted in particular." See P. Brent, *Godmen of India* (Harmondsworth: Penguin, 1973), 22.
2. For a comprehensive historical discussion of the evolution of the guru institution, on which this introductory section is based, see R.M. Steinmann, *Guru-Sisya Sambandha: Das Meister-Schuler Verhältnis im Traditionell-en und Modernen Hinduismus* (Wiesbaden: Franz Steiner, 1986). See further W. Cenker, *A Tradition of Teachers: Sankara and the Jagadgurus Today* (Delhi: Motilal Banarsidas, 1983).
3. Cenker, *Tradition of Teachers*, 41.
4. Cited in D. Gold, *The Lord as Guru* (Delhi: Oxford University Press, 1987), 104.
5. Cited in Steinmann, *Guru-Sisya Sambandha*, 87.
6. Ibid., 103.
7. L. Babb, *Redemptive Encounters* (Delhi: Oxford University Press, 1987), 218.
8. *Kulanirvana Tantra*, cited in Steinmann, 103.
9. S. Abhayananda, *Jnaneshvar* (Naples, FL: Atma Books, 1989), 122–23.
10. See, for instance, Chaturvedi Badrinath, "Sense and Nonsense about the 'Guru' Concept," *Times of India*, 13 February 1990.
11. Steinmann, *Guru-Sisya Sambandha*, 188–89.
12. Swami Saradananda, *Sri Ramakrishna, The Great Master*, 2 vols. (Mylapore: Sri Ramakrishna Math, 1983), vol. 1, 521.
13. Jayakar, *Krishnamurti*, 4.
14. Ibid., 5.
15. Ibid., 211.
16. See S. Kakar, *Shamans, Mystics and Doctors* (New York: Knopf, 1982), chap. 5.
17. S. Kakar, *The Inner World: A Psychoanalytic Study of Childhood and Society in India* (Delhi: Oxford University Press, 1978), chap. 4.
18. See H. Kohut, *The Analysis of the Self* (New York: International

Notes

Universities Press, 1971), and *The Restoration of the Self* (New York: International Universities Press, 1977).

19. Ernest Wolf, *Treatment of the Self* (New York: Guilford, 1989), 52.

20. See A. Deutsch, "Tenacity of Attachment to a Cult Leader: A Psychiatric Perspective," *American Journal of Psychiatry* 137 (1982): 1569–73. See also S. Lorand, "Psychoanalytic Therapy of Religious Devotees," *International Journal of Psychoanalysis* 43 (1962): 50–55.

21. Wolf, *Treatment of the Self*, 100.

22. S. Nacht, "Curative Factors in Psychoanalysis," *International Journal of Psychoanalysis* 43 (1962): 208. See also S.M. Abend, "Unconscious Fantasy and Theories of Cure," *Journal of the American Psychoanalytic Association* 27 (1979): 579–96.

23. Cited in Steinmann, *Guru-Sisya Sambandha*, 36.

24. Swami Satyanand Saraswati, *Light on the Guru and Disciple Relationship* (Munger: Bihar School of Yoga, 1983), 92.

25. Ibid., 77.

26. William James, *The Varieties of Religious Experience* (New York: Longmans, Green, 1902), 107, 195.

27. Cited in D. Nurbaksh, "Sufism and Psychoanalysis," *International Journal of Social Psychiatry* 24 (1978): 208.

28. Swami Muktananda, *The Perfect Relationship* (Ganesh-puri: Gurudev Siddha Vidyapeeth, 1983), ix.

29. Saradananda, *Sri Ramakrishna*, 454.

30. Muktananda, *Perfect Relationship*, 35.

31. Ibid., viii.

32. Christopher Bollas, "The Transformational Object," *International Journal of Psychoanalysis* 60 (1978): 97–107.

33. Muktananda, *Perfect Relationship*, 4.

34. Steinmann, *Guru-Sisya Sambandha*, 290.

35. Muktananda, *Perfect Relationship*, 85.

36. Babb, *Redemptive Encounters*, 173.

37. Jayakar, *Krishnamurti*, 3.

38. Cited in Steinmann, *Guru-Sisya Sambandha*, 235.

39. Ibid., 234.

40. M.L. Moeller, "Self and Object in Countertransference," *International Journal of Psychoanalysis* 58 (1977): 356–76.

41. S. Kakar, "Psychoanalysis and Religious Healing: Siblings or Strangers?" *Journal of the American Academy of Religion* 53, no. 3 (1985).

42. Muktananda, *Perfect Relationship*, 37.

43. Ibid., 109.

44. Jayakar, *Krishnamurti*, 8.

45. S.L. Bady, "The Voice as a Curative Factor in Psychotherapy," *Psychoanalytic Review* 72 (1989): 677–90.

46. S. Kakar, *Shamans, Mystics and Doctors*, 129–30.

47. Muktananda, *Perfect Relationship*, 3.
48. Moeller, "Self and Object," 373.

Chapter 3

1. E.L. Meng and E. Freud, ed., *Psychoanalysis and Faith: The Letters of Sigmund Freud and Oskar Pfister* (New York: Basic Books, 1963), 117.

2. E. Jones, *The Life and Work of Sigmund Freud*, 3 vols. (London: Hogarth Press, 1957), vol. 3.

3. Sigmund Freud, *The Future of an Illusion* (1927), Standard Edition of the Works of Sigmund Freud (London: Hogarth Press, 1953–74), vol. 21. Hereafter referred to as *Standard Edition*. Also *Civilization and Its Discontents*, *Standard Edition*, vol. 21.

4. S. Freud, *Obsessive Actions and Religious Practices* (1907), *Standard Edition*, vol. 9.

5. Wilhelm Reich, *The Function of the Orgasm* (New York: Argone Institute, 1942).

6. S. Freud, *Obsessive Actions*.

7. Franz Alexander, "Buddhistic Training as an Artificial Catatonia," *Psychoanalysis* 19 (1931): 129–45.

8. J.M. Masson, *The Oceanic Feeling: The Origins of Religious Sentiment in Ancient India* (Dordrecht: Reidel, 1980).

9. P. Ricouer, *Freud and Philosophy,* trans. Denis Savage (New Haven: Yale University Press, 1970), 533.

10. Erik H. Erikson, *Young Man Luther* (New York: Norton, 1958), 264.

11. Bruno Bettelheim, *Freud and Man's Soul* (New York: Knopf, 1983).

12. Karen Horney, *Neurosis and Human Growth* (New York: Norton, 1950), 35.

13. Erich Fromm, *Psychoanalysis and Religion* (New Haven: Yale University Press, 1950).

14. A. Kaplan, "Maturity in Religion," *Bulletin of the Philadelphia Association for Psychoanalysis* 13 (1963): 101–19; H. Guntrip, "Religion in Relation to Personal Interaction," *British Journal of Medical Psychology* 42 (1969): 323–33; Peter Homans, *Theology after Freud* (Indianapolis: Bobbs-Merrill, 1970).

15. Ricouer, *Freud and Philosophy*, 548–49.

16. Jacob Arlow, "Ego Psychology and the Study of Mythology," *Journal of the American Psychoanalytic Association* 9 (1961): 371–93.

17. Erikson, *Young Man Luther*, 264.

18. Gregory Zilboorg, *Freud and Religion: A Restatement* (London: Chapman, 1958).

19. Meng and E. Freud, *Psychoanalysis and Faith*, 133.

20. See H.P. Jung, "The Prototype of Pre-oedipal Reconstruction," *Journal of the American Psychoanalytic Association* 25 (1977): 757–85; Irving B. Harrison, "On Freud's View of the Infant-Mother Relationship and of the

Oceanic Feeling—Some Subjective Influences," *Journal of the American Psychoanalytic Association* 27 (1979): 399–421.

21. Harrison, "Some Subjective Influences."

22. S. Freud, *Moses and Monotheism* (1939), *Standard Edition*, vol. 23, 134.

23. Harrison, "Some Subjective Influences." 420.

24. Ibid., 402.

25. E. Jones, *Life and Work of Freud*, vol. 3, 392.

26. Harrison, "Some Subjective Influences," 418–19.

27. Peter Homans, *The Ability to Mourn* (Chicago: University of Chicago Press, 1989).

28. S. Freud, *The Psychopathology of Everyday Life, Standard Edition*, vol. 6, 2.

29. Cited in David S. Berman, "Stefan Zweig and His Relationship with Freud and Rolland," *International Review of Psychoanalysis* 6 (1979): 85.

30. George Steiner, "A Note on Language and Psychoanalysis," *International Review of Psychoanalysis* 3 (1976): 257.

31. Meng and E. Freud, *Psychoanalysis and Faith*, 126.

32. W.R. Bion, *Attention and Interpretation* (London: Tavistock, 1970), 62.

33. For a survey of the various relational theories in psychoanalysis, see J.R. Greenberg and S.A. Mitchell, *Object Relations in Psychoanalytic Theory* (Cambridge, MA: Harvard University Press, 1983). For an important exploration of religion and religious experience from the viewpoint of relational theories, especially the work of Winnicott, see W.W. Meissner, *Psychoanalysis and Religious Experience* (New Haven: Yale University Press, 1984).

34. D.W. Winnicott, *Playing and Reality* (London: Tavistock, 1971), 1–25.

35. Ibid., 14.

36. Winnicott, *Playing and Reality*, 96.

37. Erikson, *Young Man Luther*, 263–64.

38. H. Kohut, *Self Psychology and the Humanities* (New York: Norton, 1985).

39. S. Kakar, "Psychoanalysis and Religious Healing: Siblings or Strangers?" *Journal of the American Academy of Religion* 53, no. 3 (1985).

40. Ava L. Siegler, "The Oedipus Myths and the Oedipus Complex: Intersecting Realm, Shared Structures," *International Review of Psychoanalysis* 10 (1983): 205–14.

41. Ibid., 206.

42. Oliver Sacks, *The Man Who Mistook His Wife for a Hat* (New York: Harper and Row, 1987).

43. Bion, *Attention and Interpretation*. See also M. Milner, "Some Notes on Psychoanalytic Ideas about Mysticism," in *The Suppressed Madness of Sane Men* (London: Routledge, 1989), 257–71.

Index

Index